Praise for Dr. Anthony Wolf's
"Get Out of My Life, but First Could You
Drive Me and Cheryl to the Mall?"

"The title of this wonderful book reveals at once that Dr. Wolf does more than listen to young people. He hears them and then goes beyond their protestations and pleading to provide us with an understanding of their lives. Without piety, self-righteousness, or arrogance, he offers assistance and advice for living with, dare I even say raising, our teens in a loving and compassionate manner."

—THOMAS J. COTTLE, Ph.D.
Massachusetts School of
Professional Psychology

"Dr. Wolf empathizes with parents, does not belittle teens, and makes both wonderfully human. *Get Out of My Life* has Spock's common sense, the insight of Freud, and the wit of Bombeck. I welcome this book."

—DOROTHY M. ZEISER, Ph.D.
Chairman, Department of Child Study
Education and Special Education,
Saint Joseph College

"I love this book! It is easy to read, practical, and while putting the needs of the children first understands the instincts of parents."

—KATHY LYNN
Parenting Today

Also by Anthony E. Wolf, Ph.D.

———

*"Get out of my life, but first
could you drive me and Cheryl to the mall?":*
A Parent's Guide to the New Teenager

*"It's not fair, Jeremy Spencer's parents
let him stay up all night!":*
A Guide to the Tougher Parts of Parenting

*"Why did you have to get a divorce?
And when can I have a hamster?":*
A Guide to Parenting Through Divorce

The Secret of Parenting: How to Be in Charge
of Today's Kids—from Toddlers to
Preteens—Without Threats or Punishment

"Mom, Jason's Breathing on Me!"

The Solution to Sibling Bickering

Anthony E. Wolf, Ph.D.

BALLANTINE BOOKS · NEW YORK

A Ballantine Book
Published by The Random House Publishing Group
Copyright © 2003 by Tony Wolf

www.ballantinebooks.com

Library of Congress Cataloging-in-Publication Data

Wolf, Anthony E.
    "Mom, Jason's breathing on me!" : the solution to sibling
bickering / Anthony E. Wolf.—1st ed.
        p.   cm.
    1. Sibling rivalry. 2. Child rearing. I. Title.

    BF723.S43W65 2003
    649'.143—dc21

                                        2003045347

ISBN 0-345-46092-8

Book design by Julie Schroeder

Cover illustration by Neal McPheeters

Manufactured in the United States of America

First Edition: September 2003

10 9 8 7 6 5 4 3 2 1

To Nick and Margaret

Contents

Acknowledgments

I would like to thank Cynthia Merman who edited my manuscript and helped make a book whose words were mine but somehow came out better. I would like to thank my editor at Ballantine, Elisabeth Kallick Dyssegaard. Now into our second decade together, she has been an ongoing pleasure to work with and a wonderful support. Also, as always, my agent, Joe Spieler, for his consistent enthusiasm and his wisdom in steering me in good directions.

I want to thank Diane Nadeau for her amazing readiness to type whatever I gave her and for her very encouraging enjoyment of what she typed. I want to thank Ken Talan for his enthusiastic help in tracking down a reference. Also McDonald's and Starbucks where this book was written and where not once did anyone hassle the older gentleman with his piles of papers.

I want to thank my two ever-available readers, my friend Hugh Conlon and my wife, Mary Alice. I do not know how the book could have been written without their constant support and input. I want to thank my two sisters, Mary and Ellen, for having participated in the same childhood as I did, and having become wonderful friends and supports in my adult life. Last I want to thank my children, Nick and Margaret, for having been a consistent source of joy in my life.

"Mom, Jason's Breathing on Me!"

Introduction

"Mom, Roger won't stay on his side of the couch."

"But Angie's hogging the whole thing."

"Dad, Debbie took my monkey pillow and won't give it back."

"I did not. Benji's a big fat liar."

Sibling bickering can take more joy out of parenting than probably any other aspect of child raising. This is a book about sibling bickering—why it happens, what it means, and especially what to do about it. This book offers a very specific solution that works—for you and your children, for any parents and children. It is a solution that has the power to make the whole process of child raising dramatically more pleasant.

I am a practicing child psychologist and the father of two—now grown—children. I wrote this book because the method of dealing with sibling bickering that I describe here is one I used myself, recommended to others, and observed the results. It is simple and *it works*.

The Perfect Parent

"Mommy, Nicole says that she's going to flush my drawing down the toilet."

"I did not! The little baby. She's taking all my Magic Markers."

"But you said I could use them."

"I did not, you liar."

Simultaneously: "Mommmmm!"

"Both of you, just calm down. Let's go to the thinking corner. Ashley, you sit here. Nicole, you sit there. Now each of you, one at a time, and what's the big rule?"

"No interrupting."

"Right. Now each of you, one at a time, no interrupting, tell me what happened. Then let's see if we can work out some kind of solution. But remember about solutions— neither of you will get exactly what you want. Ashley, you go first."

Though it was hard for the girls not to interrupt each other, Ashley told her side of the story. Then Nicole told hers. Next, the two children and their mother—in a relatively short time—hashed out a solution. During the process the girls' mother did not so much offer suggestions as encourage the girls to come up with the ideas on their own. In the end the solution they came up with, just as their mother had said, was not 100 percent acceptable to either girl, but it was a solution that they could both live with.

The girls went back to playing, their disagreement now

behind them. Their mother was happy. The bickering had ended, and the girls had been able again to work out a resolution to their conflict with a minimum of help from her. The mother smiled.

Then she awoke from her pleasant daydream.

"The thinking corner? I hate the thinking corner. Ashley always lies."

"I do not. You're the big liar."

"Mom, Ashley called me a liar."

"Mom, it's not fair. Just because Ashley's a little baby she gets everything. I'm gonna kill you, Ashley."

"Mom, Nicole says she's going to kill me."

Where did I go wrong? wondered their mother.

The pleasant daydream just described is more or less what we all feel the perfect parent is supposed to do in response to sibling bickering. And if you *are* a perfect parent, your children will respond to your perfect-parent behavior by moving toward positive character-building resolutions of conflicts. Conversely, if you are unable to follow the above pattern, you are being less than a perfect parent, maybe far less.

The flaw in all of this—and it is a huge flaw—is that in reality you are dealing with human children who are not afraid of their parents. With today's children, the just-described perfect parent behavior is not perfect at all—because it will not work. Not only will it not work, but with the overwhelming majority of siblings the overwhelming majority of the time it is unhelpful, producing only negative results. The old model—the one we all think of as the ideal—doesn't apply. Today's kids are different from kids in the past, and parenting is different. Parents today need a whole new approach.

A New World of Parenting

An eight-year-old boy comes to school.

"Where did you get that bruise, Jimmy?" asks his teacher, noticing a large black-and-blue mark on the side of his face.

"My mom hit me."

In every state in the United States today, state law mandates that a teacher has to report the bruise to child abuse authorities.

In the 1930s:

"Where did you get that bruise, Jimmy?" asks his teacher.

"My mom hit me."

"Boy, you must have done something pretty bad," responds his teacher.

Back then not all teachers would have responded this way, but they might have. Seventy years ago there were no laws that anybody had to report anything to anyone.

One outstanding fact probably more than any other has shaped how children today behave with their parents. Over the past two generations there has come a revolution in child-raising practice that has totally transformed the parent–child relationship. The use of harsh punishment—hard smacks on the face, getting out the switch or the belt, locking a child in a room for an extended period of time—is no longer considered acceptable. Though some parents may still use them, there is now ingrained in our parenting culture a line past which parents may not go. The result—a gigantic result—is that kids today, in a way that simply did not exist in the past, are not afraid of their parents.

I am talking about real fear. Not about fear that you will get yelled at by an angry parent, that you will be grounded, that you won't get to watch TV. I am talking about the fear that something *really* bad will happen to you. I am a strong believer that the elimination of real fear from child raising is a great step forward for humankind. It put into the culture and into the children who were its beneficiaries the idea that serious parent-inflicted suffering has no place in child raising. Real fear as part of child raising makes for a more, not less, violent world. But as a result, one major inhibition on children's behavior with their parents, an inhibition that had existed over the previous centuries, is gone. How do children who are not afraid of their parents act?

"Jeremy, please hang up your jacket."

"But it's not fair. Why do I always have to do stuff and Jennifer never has to do anything? Besides, my arm hurts. It does. I think maybe I broke it."

They talk back. You tell them to do something that they don't feel like doing, and they usually obey, but often only after—sometimes extended—fussing. As I discuss later, for a number of reasons this behavior is not nearly as bad as it seems. But the bottom line: With the removal of real fear, a historic restraint on child behavior with their parents is gone.

No interrupting? Hardly.

"If either of you interrupts, I swear on Grandma Nana's grave that I will do terrible things to you. Look at me. I really mean it."

"No, you won't. You're just saying that. You won't because you love us, and besides you'd have to go to jail forever."

Fear created a line past which children hesitated to go lest they suffer dire consequences. Without fear, shutting up and not pleading your case when your sibling is building an intolerable-to-listen-to and totally false case against you is not something that is going to happen.

Think about an argument with someone to whom you are very close—boyfriend, girlfriend, spouse—and he or she is accusing you of something that is totally wrong, wildly misrepresenting events, getting it completely backward. Indeed, it is the other person, not you, who is at fault. Do you patiently sit and listen to the full recitation of this absolute slander and then say your piece?

"Gosh, James, all that you just said over the last twenty minutes—I might add, in a loud and unpleasant manner—I see quite differently from you."

So who are today's children? They feel free to act like children, which is very good. But obviously they are not as easy to manage as in the old days when fear held sway. As to the ideal parent response to sibling bickering, we all operate under a model that is a delusion. The model applies only to a world that no longer exists.

This is a book about real children—who they are, what they want, why they act as they do, and what you can do about it. But before I offer my solution to sibling bickering, I need to talk about one fact about children that underlies all that I recommend.

What All Children Want Most

Eight-year-old Kendra was sitting on the floor of the family kitchen and dining area working on an intricate building project with her Construct-O-Straws. Over by the kitchen sink, her father was chopping vegetables for a big pot of soup. So engrossed was Kendra in her building project that for the past twenty minutes, she had not once looked over at her father.

A question: Assuming that Kendra is a human child, what would have to happen that she would *immediately* abandon her project and start demanding attention from her father? I ask this question with the absolute knowledge that you, my reader, know the answer. I want to emphasize that we are talking about a universal fact of nature, a primary immutable natural law.

What would need to happen that Kendra would immediately stop working with her Construct-O-Straws and start pestering her father?

The phone rang.

"Dad, look at what I'm building."

"In a minute, Kendra. I'm on the phone."

"But you have to look at it. It's really good."

"Kendra, I am on the phone. In a minute."

"But you have to look at it. You *never* look at my stuff."

"Kendra, you know that's not true. I will. Later. I am on the phone."

"But it won't be the same later."

"Kendra! *I am on the phone!*"

What was Kendra's problem? Why this sudden passion to get her father's attention when for the last twenty minutes she'd had no interest in showing him her building project or interacting with him in any way at all? What internal force, triggered by the phone, suddenly unleashed such a passion for her father's attention, a passion that had been so totally dormant only a few seconds earlier? For the previous twenty minutes as Kendra sat on the floor playing with her Construct-O-Straws, her project held her full interest. She had no need of her father's attention. But once the phone rang, this immediately jeopardized a deal that all along had been there, necessary for Kendra's contentment in order to focus on her building project. Lying just below the surface, but necessary for her full happiness, was the knowledge that *No, I don't want my father's attention now, but* should *I want his attention, it must be immediately and fully available.*

There is a part in all children that wants not just love, nurturing, understanding, that craves not just emotional sustenance, but instead wants everything. Everything is all of you, every little bit.

This craving is normal. It comes as part of the healthy love attachment that children make to their parents in earliest childhood. As a result of this attachment, parents and only parents become the sole source of an incredible richness. It is love, which in its most desired form is *I want to engulf and be engulfed by my beloved.* It is an inevitable side of love. There is a part of them that does not want only what they need; it wants everything, totally, on demand.

There exists in all children a desire not just for some of a parent but all of parent. Every possible bit.

What would Kendra's father have to do to satisfy Kendra?

"I'm sorry, Karl. I can't talk now. Kendra wants me to look at her Construct-O-Straws project. I'll have to get back to you. Bye."

Now addressing Kendra: "I'm sorry, dear. How thoughtless of me not to have disconnected the phone. Of course, let me see your project."

Now Kendra, back in control of the source of attention, would probably lose interest in telling her father about her project, preferring to get back to working on it on her own. All she cared about was having full control of parent attention, even when she didn't exactly want it.

Imagine a slightly different example. Kendra is on the floor playing with her Construct-O-Straws. Her father is cutting up the vegetables. But instead of the phone ringing, her very quiet five-year-old sister Anyssa comes into the room and silently stands against the wall watching her. Their father, intent on chopping vegetables, has not yet even noticed that Anyssa has come into the room. Yet the same will happen as with the phone ringing. *As soon as* Anyssa comes into the room, Kendra drops what she is doing and starts at her father.

"See what I've made."

Kendra cannot bear the possibility that her father might pay some attention to Anyssa. Kendra has to preempt that risk, striking first so she can fully control the source of parent attention.

Parents often comment that their child may be content to play alone, but as soon as a spouse comes home, suddenly their child loses all capacity for independent play and cannot tolerate that the two parents talk to each other.

She's so good when it's just me and her. But when it's the three of us, she gets so demanding.

An absolute fact of parenting and childhood is that the mere physical presence of a parent brings out this insatiable craving in a child. How much parent love does a child need? There *is* such a thing as enough. But as far as children are concerned, anything less than everything is not enough.

A child's wish for total attention from a parent does not depend on the existence of a sibling. The pigginess is already there. This means that when siblings bicker between themselves, if a parent gets at all involved—in any way enters the equation—just by the parent's presence, the issue that was between the siblings, whatever it was, automatically disappears. For now there is a bigger fish to go after.

It is this inevitable and insatiable pigginess for parent

that dominates any situation in which siblings bicker and a parent chooses to get involved. Picture baby piranhas fighting over an uninteresting scrap; then a peacemaker enters the scene—who also happens to be the biggest, most delicious piece of meat that ever was.

In regard to sibling bickering, where a parent is at all part of the equation, just that fact invariably brings out in children the part of them that is not looking for solutions at all, but wants *all* of you.

This is the underlying basis of what I recommend in this book, and it is why what I recommend works. But what follows did not originate from any great understanding of child psychology on my part. It came from an altogether different source, far more immediate and personal.

My Sisters and I, or the Siblings from Hell

I was the middle child between two sisters. Mary was two years younger; Ellen, two years older. We were fortunate children. Our parents were kind and loving, genuinely good people who very much wanted to do the right thing by their children. I believe that as a direct result of this, my two sisters and I grew into who we have become—good and loving adults. So much of what my parents did with me and my sisters, because I believe it was right, became the core of what I did as a parent. But there was one small area where perhaps my parents didn't quite get it.

Throughout our adult lives, my sisters and I have been

friends, supportive of each other. We have a nice relationship, which we enjoy. But when we were growing up, there was not a place that we could go, a room that we could be in, without constant squabbling. And I mean *constant*. We argued over everything. Every argument escalated into screaming and crying. Our frustrated parents were forever dragged into the middle, but with scant success at any resolution. It was over everything, all the time, without letup. Ellen and I did not actually fight with each other that much, but we weren't particularly close, either. This was mainly because we were so busy fighting with Mary, who had the huge advantage—for getting our parents on her side—of being younger, smaller, and weaker.

I remember an event also recalled by both of my sisters; it must have made quite an impression on all of us. It was a family vacation driving trip (the one and only)—we were possibly nine, eleven, and thirteen years old at the time. The trip was from Philadelphia, where we grew up, to Virginia to visit historic points of interest: Monticello, the home of Thomas Jefferson; Mount Vernon, George Washington's home; and probably some other stops I don't remember. Coming back, we took a scenic detour so that we could travel along the famous Shenandoah Skyline Drive.

As I am writing this, I have in front of me a current road map of Virginia. The Skyline Drive is still there—110 miles between Waynesboro and Front Royal, only two crossroads along its full length (were these crossroads even there fifty years ago?), and very definitely when we drove on it no rest stops. None. Nothing but scenery and a cliff dropping off on one side of the road. Of course, when we were on it, there was little scenery because the valley and the drive were engulfed in fog. One hundred and ten twisty, slowly driven miles trapped in a car with the three Wolf children. I have always felt that my father, who did most of the driving, was a true hero, a man of great strength and courage. That this book is being written attests to the fact that he did not at any point along the drive simply make a sharp right turn into the billowing fog and peaceful abyss beneath.

I suppose there are brothers and sisters who more deservedly than Mary, Ellen, and I can lay claim to the title Siblings from Hell, but if so, let them come forward.

A clear and repeating memory from my childhood is of our very wonderful and loving mother standing there in a state verging on tears, crying out, "God, give me strength." Strength to do what? Deal with three privileged, spoiled, and bratty little kids?

The years of constant bickering were not fun. Not for my parents, not for Mary, Ellen, or me. It was as a direct result of my very clear memory of my childhood that I determined I did not want my children to be a repeat of my sisters and me. My parents did most things right, but in regard to sibling bickering they were at a loss. I wanted to do something different. This was the one place in the raising of my two children that I wanted to have a concrete plan. My wife, Mary Alice, and I talked about it when Nick and Margaret were very young. We came up with such a plan. The plan started early; we began to implement it when Nick was four and Margaret was two. I do not remember what Mary Alice and I said. I don't remember the exact nature of our original, agreed-upon plan. But what evolved swiftly and remained in place throughout the rest of Nick's and Margaret's childhoods, I remember well. The plan was very clear. And very simple.

1. → The Solution to Sibling Bickering

Mary Alice and I—What We Did

We had a three-part plan.

1. If we intervened in squabbling between Nick and Margaret, it would *never* be on one side or the other. "The two of you stop it." The one and only exception was if there was potential harm to one or the other (and *harm* does not mean only pain).

2. The point in the squabbling at which we would intervene was as soon as we started to get irritated.

3. We would never listen to what went on. And I mean *never*. Again, the only exception was if there was potential harm to one or the other child.

That was it. Those were the rules. And they worked. And

because they worked, we kept using them. The results were spectacular. Nick and Margaret bickered, but what made all the difference for Mary Alice and me was that we did not get the constant, "Nicky kicked my sticker album." "I did not, she put it down right where I was sitting." "I did not. Besides he's not the boss of the TV room." "Mom, she's lying." "Nicky, you're a liar." "Dad, he's going to hit me."

We didn't get any of that because from early on both Nick and Margaret learned that if they came to us with their bickering, what they would get—always—was nothing. So they did not include us, because there was no reason to.

One gigantic benefit of our procedure was that it eliminated, absolutely and wholly removed, the number one cause of sibling rivalry: trying to get a parent on your side. We wouldn't do it. We refused to enter that arena. The great parental courtroom to which grievances are taken and final judgment made of who was right and who was wrong, the court that is such a huge part of virtually all childhoods, certainly mine, that court, the judgment from which engenders such sibling passion, for Nick and Margaret was empty. The judge wasn't there. There was no judge.

Nick and Margaret had many disagreements, the same disagreements all siblings have. But the disagreements were about whatever they were disagreeing about: who is hogging too much of the seat, who gets the slightly broken cookie, who gets to use the red Magic Marker, intrusion on each other's space. What the disagreements were never about was on whose side Mary Alice or I would be. That element, parent favor or not, never came into the disagreements, was not a part of them. *In their disagreements, a parent was not even part of the equation.*

And since it was impossible to get a parent on your side—nor could your sibling get your parent on his or her side—grievances between the two were limited to the specifics of day to day. The heart of true enmity between siblings was absent. Parent favor was never on the table.

The constant sibling squabbling that can wear you down and so totally drain the fun and any pleasure out of time spent with your children didn't exist. We were out of the loop. The squabbling that did occur was not the stomach-tightening *Oh, no, here they go again,* with whatever peace you had at any given moment instantly replaced by that familiar tension. This was *not* part of our raising of Nick and Margaret.

One thing that I can say as an absolute fact is that when they were growing up, being with Nick and Margaret was fun. I know. I was there. I do remember. Maybe not always, maybe not all the time, but overwhelmingly being with them was fun. Maybe this is a tribute to them, their personalities when growing up. Maybe it was because of what else Mary Alice and I did or did not do as parents. But I also have no doubt that a major part of the enjoyableness of Nick and Margaret, how we could go places, be places with them, so different from when I was growing up, was the direct benefit of our system of dealing with sibling squabbling. Not only were we wholly out of the loop, but they—because they had no choice, no alternative—were forced to get a lot of practice at working things out on their own.

When Nick and Margaret were little, there was a television set in a small sitting area that was an extension of our kitchen. On Saturdays they were allowed to watch kid TV programs from whenever they woke up until noon. One TV, two kids. My memory is that only once in the history of their Saturday-morning TV watching was there squabbling that resulted in our having to intervene, at which point the TV watching ended for that morning. My memory may not be totally accurate, but I will vouch that interventions were exceedingly rare. Somehow, for four hours every Saturday morning, Nick and Margaret worked out on their own, without major squabbling, which programs they would watch. What was their system? I have no idea.

Try this one. One summer when Margaret was five and Nick was seven, I was between jobs and Mary Alice was a high school teacher. We decided to take a seven-week family vacation driving in a station wagon (it was before the era of vans) around the West, mainly Colorado and California. In three days I drove by myself from Springfield, Massachusetts, to Denver, where I met Mary Alice, Nick, and Margaret, who had flown there. Then we headed out. Seven weeks driving through the West, camping or periodically staying in motels (one room).

Seven weeks in a station wagon—did I mention that it had no air-conditioning? At one point driving through Arizona, seeing Nick lying asleep in the back of the station wagon, sweat in little beads over his pink face, I thought that we had accidentally roasted him. Seven weeks in a station wagon with the Wolf kids.

We had a good time. Nick and Margaret were easy. Even very easy. There was arguing, but by far the most serious and most frequent offenders were not the children.

Rule 1: Don't Take Sides

Let me describe the rules in more detail.

Rule 1: Never intervene on one side or the other unless there is possible harm.

Maurice was putting away dishes while watching TV when high-pitched screaming erupted. Going into the next room, he beheld his seven-year-old son Louis sitting on five-year-old Lainie, hitting her on the back. The screaming was coming from Lainie because she was being sat upon and hit on the back by her brother.

Rule 1 says never intervene on one side or the other unless there is possible harm. By *harm* I mean the possibility of causing injury, not minor pain. Maurice has to make a swift decision. Does he feel that what Louis is doing to his sister could result in possible harm? Let's say he decides that his seven-year-old son beating on the back of his five-year-old daughter does not represent a serious threat of injury. Then his intervention must be, "The two of you, stop it, now."

If Louis does not immediately stop and get off Lainie, Maurice must remove Louis from atop his sister. If Maurice decides that there is no potential harm, Rule 1 says he should not intervene on one side or the other. He does *not* say, "Louis, stop hitting your sister."

By saying, "The two of you stop it," and pulling Louis off his sister if he does not immediately stop hitting, Maurice has accomplished what is necessary. The hitting has now stopped and no side has been taken.

On the other hand, should he say, "Louis, stop hitting your sister," he is taking a side.

What he will get is, "But Lainie messed up my cars and she was pinching me."

"I did not. Louis never lets me play with anything."

"I do too, but you mess everything up."

Saying, "Louis stop hitting your sister," adds nothing. Louis knows perfectly well that he is not supposed to hit his sister. Regardless, his father's intervention has stopped the hitting. If the squabbling then ends, Maurice needs to do no more. He can return to what he was doing. All "Louis, stop hitting your sister" adds is an argument.

Better, if there is no threat of harm: "The two of you, stop it, now."

The squabbling may continue—often it will. Maybe Louis and Lainie keep yelling at each other, or one or the other wants to keep the physical fight going.

Hands clawed, Lainie rushes at her brother, shouting, "Make him stop hitting me," even though the hitting has stopped. (Six months previously she had perfected the Pinch of Death.)

Separation

As soon as it is apparent that the squabbling is going to continue—even if it is only one child who is persisting—separation becomes necessary. Where squabbling does not stop, separation is always the immediate next step.

"I'm not doing anything," insists Louis, who has backed off.

"Okay, that's it. Lainie, you're going to be in the kitchen with me."

The separation can take any form, so long as they are no longer together. Lainie in the kitchen. Or Louis in the kitchen. Both temporarily banished to their rooms, if they have separate rooms. Each on separate sides of a room. The specifics do not matter. The point is that brother and sister—for now—are separated.

"But it's not fair. I want to be in the TV room," screams Lainie. "Why does Louis get to stay in the TV room?"

When separating siblings, you do not want to worry too much about fairness. Over time fairness will work itself out. Speed, not fairness, is your main aim. The children's father, not responding to Lainie's complaint, guides her into the kitchen.

"But it's not fair."

Sometimes who should be separated to where is obvious. One child is in another's room. Or one child is set up in a specific place working on a particular project.

"That's it, the two of you. The squabbling stops. Lainie,

you're going to have to go somewhere else while Louis is working on his art project."

But more often than not, you just need to act fast and not worry about fairness.

The separation is temporary. They will be allowed back together again, in this case Lainie returning to the TV room. When? There is no set rule. Basically when you judge that things have calmed down enough so that they can be trusted back together without immediate resumption of squabbling. But as a parent of human children, you cannot reasonably hope that the squabbling will cease forever. If they are together, squabbling is always a possibility. And no, the solution is not to keep them separate all the time.

"No, Lainie, you know you can be only on the blue-painted side of the house."

"But why does Louis always get the red side? It's not fair. He has the only two bathrooms."

If back together they resume squabbling, again they will have to be separated. But they get the message that this is standard policy. Squabbling—if it reaches a certain decibel level—produces swift parent intervention and separation.

As a result, they build in controls. *Unless I want to take my chances on being removed altogether, I can't get too wild being mad at Carly.* They develop self-monitoring. But even with self-monitoring, on rainy nonschool days, the above may be a procedure that is carried out often.

If There Is Threat of Harm

But let's say there was threat of harm. Let's say that Louis was choking Lainie or about to hit her on the head with a wooden block. Then the intervention has to be different. Maurice must immediately stop Louis. But then—in those instances where there is the possibility of harm—he must focus directly on the one who could be causing harm, in this case Louis. It is for such situations of possible harm that you want to reserve your sternest voice:

"You cannot choke your sister. You cannot hurt her. You can never choke."

"But she scratched me real hard."

Which, let us assume, is true. Still, Louis's father cannot be deflected from his very important message.

"You cannot choke your sister. Ever."

The message is a very basic one: Harming is never okay. There are no reasons that make it okay. Harm can never be allowed to happen.

And later, because potential harm is serious business, Maurice should go to Louis and say, "This afternoon, you were choking Lainie. You can never do that." And he could then explain why choking can be harmful.

The message is simple. *Of everything in the world, what I, your parent whom you love and who loves you, feel the most strongly about is possible harm. It must not happen.*

Another benefit to responding on one side only when there is threat of harm is that it strongly emphasizes the most important message: *Harm is the most serious of all transgressions.*

Let's say that Maurice came in and saw Louis sitting on Lainie, hitting her on the back. But then Lainie reached out and picked up a solid metal fire truck and was about to give her brother a backhanded bash with it. Solid metal fire trucks can cause harm. They should not be used as weapons in a fight. Hence: "No, Lainie, put down the fire truck." And Maurice takes it out of her hand if she does not immediately put it down.

Then, directly addressing Lainie in a very serious manner, even while he may now be pulling Louis off his sister: "No, Lainie, the fire truck could really hurt Louis. You cannot hit with it."

"But he is hitting me."

"You cannot hit with a fire truck."

The message to Lainie: *There is something about hitting with the fire truck that is really serious, far more so than Louis sitting on you and hitting your back. Something especially bad. It is* harm.

Louis is impressed, too. He was hitting his sister, and not only does he not get yelled at, she does. *Hitting with the fire truck must be* really *bad. Worse than me sitting on her and hitting her on the back. It is. It can cause harm.*

It is a very good message, precisely the one you want to teach. And it's a particularly powerful teaching example because it so strongly emphasizes the exact line you want to emphasize. *Above anything, harm is the worst. It may not happen.*

———

Rule 1: Never intervene on one side or the other unless there is threat of harm. It is a good rule because—no way around it—to the extent that you choose to intervene on one side or the other, you now have placed yourself in the middle, a place that you do not want to be, because there is no escape.

"But Dad!"

"Dad, Dad, don't listen to her."

Rule 2: Act Fast (or Not at All)

Rule 2: The point at which to intervene is when you *start* to get irritated.

Jenny was kibitzing as her sister Gabriela played with her new drawing kit.

"Gabriela, that's not the right way to do it."

"It is too."

"It's not. You're doing it wrong."

"I am too doing it right."

"You're going to ruin it."

"I am not."

"You are too."

"Leave me alone."

"Gabriela, I'm just trying to help you."

"Leave me alone."

"Here, let me have it. I'll show you how."

"Let go!"

"No, Gabriela. You are doing it wrong."

"Let go!"

"No, unless you let me show you."

"Let go! Let go!"

"No. Owww! Gabriela, you little bitch!"

"Owww! Jenny!"

"You two, stop it now. I am sick and tired of the two of you fussing all the time. Can't you for once play together nicely? I am really sick of this. I mean it. I have had it with the two of you. I *really* have had it."

Lois, the girls' mother, had been sitting in the same room as the girls, going over accounts for the business that she ran out of her home. Once her children began to bicker, she found it hard to concentrate on what she was doing. She became increasingly irritated as the squabbling escalated. When she finally did intervene, she was very angry and found herself screaming at her children.

The children swiftly backed off, recognizing that their mother was seriously angry. The squabbling ended—at least for now. But Lois, having gotten angry and, on top of that, upset that she had gotten angry, needed a good ten minutes before she cooled down enough to make further headway on the work that she was doing.

Rule 2: Intervene as soon as you *start* to get irritated. When Lois first noticed that the bickering was interfering with her concentration was when she should have intervened. Very early.

"Gabriela, that's not the right way to do it."

"It is too."

"It's not. You're doing it wrong."

At that moment, if the mother noticed herself focusing on the start of her daughters' disagreement and not on her work, right there, before she even had a chance to get angry and before the fight, as well as her own temper, escalated:

"The two of you. I'm working. If you can't play quietly, I don't want you together."

"But Gabriela isn't doing it right."

"If you can't play quietly, I don't want you two together. I'm trying to work."

That early.

This is not to say that whenever siblings start to bicker you should always intervene. Sometimes it may not bother you. As I will discuss shortly, much can be gained from at times allowing the bickering to run its course.

Let's say that instead of working on her accounts, Lois was talking on the phone with her mother, engrossed in her conversation so that she was more or less oblivious to the girls' squabbling, just keeping an eye on them to make sure it didn't get too out of hand. It was not until the girls started hitting each other and screaming that she felt it intruded on her phone call.

"Excuse me, Mother."

Putting down the phone, she walked over to her daughters.

"That's it. The two of you, stop it now, or neither of you can be in here. I am trying to talk to Nene."

When should you intervene? The minute a disagreement starts? As soon as it reaches a certain degree of loudness? When it first gets physical?

What I recommend is to intervene when *you* start to get

irritated. This isn't an absolute rule. It is what I did, and I think it worked well. But some parents want no hitting and intervene as soon as any hitting starts. They take a strong stand that any hitting of a sibling is not okay.

Others may intervene when a certain decibel level has been exceeded. I like my way, but regardless, the rule is to intervene immediately once your acceptable line has been passed.

The Benefits of Bickering

At whatever point in sibling bickering you choose to intervene, it is important to bear in mind that not all sibling bickering is bad. You do not want a policy that tries to head off bickering as soon as it starts, a policy that says that all kinds of bickering are bad all the time. For one, such a policy won't work unless the children permanently live in separate homes. Bickering is bad if it leads to damage. It is bad when it intrudes on the peace of others. But there are certain very real advantages to allowing sibling bickering to play itself out—at least some of the time. One obvious advantage is that children get practice in dealing with disagreements. How hard to push. When to back off. Even strategies for compromise.

Let's say that Jenny and Gabriela's mother didn't intervene when Jenny was trying to supervise her sister's play. Who knows?—the following might have happened:

The argument between Jenny and Gabriela proceeded as described to the point where Gabriela had hit Jenny and Jenny had hit back.

"No. Owww! Gabriela, you little bitch!"

"Owww! Jenny!"

But then Jenny chose to back off.

"All right, you big baby. I don't care if you screw it up. You're such a big baby, you don't know anything."

"*You're* a big baby." And Gabriela happily resumed her drawing.

A couple of useful lessons learned.

By Jenny: *Gabriela's not always going to accept my well-meant help.*

By Gabriela: *If I persist, Jenny will stop trying to butt in and always trying to tell me what to do.*

I think the best point to intervene in sibling bickering is as soon as you start to get irritated. But you do need to have some tolerance for bickering. It can be noisy. But you do not always want to intervene. How else will they ever learn to work through anything on their own? Maybe just as important: How else will you ever learn that they can? You want to allow much of the bickering simply to play itself out.

Rule 3: Don't Listen

Rule 3: Do not listen—ever—except where there is possibility of harm.

This is a big one. Its benefits to you are enormous, and it totally changes the whole meaning and purpose of bickering between siblings, moving it in a direction far more healthy and useful.

It is not very complicated.

"Mommy, Evan called me a swear."
"I don't want to hear about it."

"Daddy, Lydia's not giving me a turn."
"I don't want to hear about it."

"Mommy, Betsy pushed me."
"I don't want to hear about it."

"Daddy, Ezra drooled on purpose on my sweater."
"I don't want to hear about it."

The rule is that you do not want to get involved in their arguments; you have no interest in hearing about their bickering. This does not mean that you cannot offer love, understanding, and sympathy. More often than not, at that point they are not so interested in love, understanding, and sympathy. But the offer is always a good one.

I'm not interested in any of that stuff. I want her to say how I'm right and go yell at Ezra and give him a big punishment.

But sometimes these offerings may be enough. They are

always a good place to start. It is never bad to validate their feelings.

"I understand how you feel. Ezra can really make you mad. (But don't think for a minute I'm going to do anything about it.)"

Actually, there are gentler and just as effective forms of "I don't want to hear about it."

"Mommy, Evan called me a swear."
"Would you like a hug?"

"Daddy, Lydia's not giving me a turn."
"Gosh, that must be frustrating."

"Mommy, Betsy pushed me."
"Gee, that must not have been pleasant."

"Daddy, Ezra drooled on purpose on my sweater."
"Golly, that sounds like a problem."

That is, *I'm happy to be understanding, sympathetic, loving, but whatever the problem is, it is a problem for you and not for me. You will have to deal with it or not, because I certainly won't. I am available for love. But the problem—I am gently, lovingly throwing that back to you.*

As mentioned, sometimes it is enough.

"Mommy, Evan called me a swear."
"Would you like a hug?"

And J. J. comes over and gets a hug.

"I hate him. I hate Evan. I'm gonna say swears back at him." Yet all the while, J. J. sucks up the hug and then happily heads off.

But as mentioned, often hugs and understanding are not what they are after.

"Mommy, Evan called me a swear."

"Would you like a hug?"

"But he called me a swear."

"Are you sure you don't want a hug?"

"But he called me a swear. You don't understand. He's not allowed to do that."

"Golly, that must have made you mad. That sounds like a problem."

"You're not listening to me."

"Gosh, J. J., I don't know what to say to you." (This is a good phrase to have handy.)

"Evan called me a swear. You have to do something. I'm going to call him a worse swear."

J. J.'s mother makes it clear to her son that she will offer love and sympathy but nothing more.

Often you can tell pretty quickly whether love and understanding may be of use, or whether the kids are out for blood—that is, getting you involved.

Hence, after J. J.'s initial rejection of a hug, probably that was the point at which his mother would want to disengage.

"Would you like a hug?"

"But he called me a swear."

"Gosh, J. J., I don't know what to say to you."

"But you have to do something. Evan called me a swear."

"You'll just have to deal with him yourself."

"But I can't. You have to."

J. J.'s mother should say no more. Any further response will only feed J. J.'s frustration.

"You're mean. I'll call him a bad swear."

And then J. J. exits, returning to deal or not with the problem on his own. Which is exactly what you want.

If you don't want love or understanding, then I have nothing else to offer.

As will be discussed, there are times for listening. But this is not one of them.

The reason not listening is such a powerful and beneficial response to sibling bickering is that it tells children that bickering, other than in regard to issues of harm, is exclusively between them; parents are not a part of it. It says that bickering, other than where there is threat of harm, is totally separate from anything to do with a parent. As discussed, because of the inevitable and good attachment of children to parents, just the presence of a parent as a part of sibling bickering automatically brings out in children the powerful and normal craving for as much parent as they can get. As soon as you become part of the equation, any rational, interested-in-possibly-working-on-resolutions part of a child disappears from the scene. In its stead is the totally mindless, ravening child whose only interest is getting all of you.

Eliminating parents as part of the sibling bickering equation, that and only that, allows children actually to work out solutions on their own. Only where parents stay out of it will sibling bickering exist in its own separate realm, a problem between them, rather than about something altogether different—getting as much of you as possible.

Working It Through on Their Own

Basic to my approach to sibling bickering is the assumption that much that goes on between children can be allowed to happen, to play itself out, without your regular supervision. It assumes that there even are benefits to allowing much to proceed without your input. There is much that is already a part of them, much of that put in by your love and attention, that enables them to deal with many of the trials and tribulations of day-to-day life—especially that of not getting their way—all on their own.

—A McDonald's story—

A boy, who looked to be about eight, was having a tantrum. I did not observe what precipitated it. Present also were his mother and his grandmother, who tried to stop the tantrum. They cajoled, threatened, tried to distract, tried to reason with the boy. Nothing worked. The tantrum got worse, almost seeming to feed off his mother's and grandmother's attempts to end it. As I sat there watching, my strong sense was of the two adults actively trying to do something—

anything—to end the tantrum. I do not remember how it ended (I think unpleasantly), but I do remember that it went on for a long time.

—Another McDonald's story—

A two- or three-year-old girl, accompanied by both of her parents, was having a fit. Again, I didn't see what it was about. The father picked up the girl, who continued crying and squirming. Beyond the father holding his daughter, neither parent seemed to pay any further attention to her, letting her fuss as they cleaned up their table. They then left the McDonald's, the girl still crying. But I could see that now, in new surroundings, the girl stopped crying and began looking around—very much acting as if the tantrum had never happened.

There is a parental strategy that says: *Where children face frustration and disappointment, we as parents should help them, giving them tools to work through their regular day-to-day disappointments.* I am not a big fan of this strategy.

I think for normal everyday frustration and disappointment, the parents' main role is to establish for their children limits as to what reactions are acceptable or not.

Draw the line between physical expression and the use of words. "Trying to kick me is not okay." "Saying, 'I hate you, you're the meanest daddy in the world,' is okay."

If their behavior is sufficiently unpleasant to be around, where possible, you will separate them and you. "If you are upset, you can be as obnoxious as you want, but not around me." *If they want hugs, I will give them. If they want understanding, I will listen. But I am not actively going to work at resolving their day-to-day frustrations for them.*

All of this relies on one assumption: If you have been a good, loving parent, as part of normal child development your children will have a basic internalized sense of good feeling, a permanent internal resource of well-being to fall back on. I have always pictured it very much like a little pot-bellied stove that lies at the core of the personality. They get this from you. In the face of normal day-to-day frustrations and disappointments, it allows them to work through the resultant bad feelings all on their own. When those bad feelings enter their bodies, all they have to do is wait. In a relatively short period of time, the bad feelings fade away. Their core of good, warm feeling gradually brings them back to feeling fine. They have the capacity to do this all within their own little heads and bodies—without any help from you. You have already done your part by giving them the good emotional nurturing.

For major problems, they need all the help from you that they can get. But for daily frustrations—especially those of not getting their way—they have inside of them the capacity to work through those problems all on their own.

I hate Mommy and I hate Daddy and I hate everybody and especially I hate Brian. I wish I had a nice family. But I don't. I have a not-nice family. They all hate me. And I never get anything I want. I'm the saddest girl in the world.

It would be better if I lived on an island with a nice family. A family that liked me. Maybe they'd all be giraffes. And they would try to lick my face and feed me leaves. But leaves are gross, so I would have to have my own food. Actually, I think giraffes are stupid, so maybe I would get bored. Actually, I'm a little bored now. I think I'll go and pester Brian some and see if I can make him have a temper tantrum.

"Brian. Where are you? I'm not mad anymore. I have a special treat for you."

Listening

I want to be heard. I want to shout my words so they echo through the mountains and the valleys. Hear me. Know my words. Know me.

Our children desperately want to be heard. Listening to them is a huge part of how we nurture them. But there are times for listening and times for not listening.

When children are not getting their way, it is not bad to listen—briefly. You can even listen and decide to change your mind based on what they are saying.

"Please, please, please let me go over to Emily's"—who lives two houses down. "I know I stayed too long yesterday, but I promise this time I'll get home before supper."

"All right, but make sure you're home by five-thirty, no later."

"Love you."

That is excellent.

But when they are not getting their way, you do not want to listen very long. For with real children, if you decide not to change your mind, they swiftly move on to the endless pleading that you know all too well. And they go on *forever.* The babyish part of them that never lets go, that keeps arguing all the way to the gates of eternity and beyond, takes over and dominates all that subsequently goes on. How many parents have ever experienced the following after half an hour of arguing back and forth with their child?

"Gosh, Mom, I don't like it, but I see where you're coming from. You let me tell my whole side of the story. I know you heard me. I'm unhappy that you're not going to change your mind. But as I said, I see where you're coming from. I don't like it, but I know I have to accept it."

So when do you listen? Any other time. Any time when there is not still an issue on the table about which your child is unhappy and about which you are not going to change your mind. Any other time but then.

How do you listen? By being there. Is there a secret to listening? No. The core of listening, how kids get to feel that they are heard, how the nurturing takes place, is that they fill the space and time between you and them with themselves.

"Dad, I really like butter cookies. Remember the ones we got from Aunt Carrie for Mom's birthday? I love them.

Except I didn't like the kind of square-shaped ones. Do you remember them?"

You can listen quietly. You can listen actively, reacting with your own thoughts about what your children say.

"I liked the square ones."

"You did! I didn't. They tasted funny."

The idea of listening is to let them tell you about what they think and feel and have them know that you hear them. One common parent problem in listening is that we have a tendency to jump in with our own agendas.

"Mom, it was so fun. Katya's swing set was so cool. I really got up high."

"Chrissa, are you sure you're careful when you do that? You know, if you fell, you could get really hurt."

"Mom, I was careful."

"I hope you remembered to thank them when you left."

"Mom!"

Hello. I was trying to tell you about how much fun I had and how cool the swing set was.

Ideally, we can keep ourselves enough in check that our children get to tell us what they want. But even when we do bring in our stuff, it is not bad—we can't help doing it. They have our attention, and they usually push through to give us what they want.

"Mom, I said thank you. I'm telling you about the swing set."

In regard to sibling bickering, the rule is that when they come to you, do not listen. But more accurately, the rule is that you do not want to listen in the role of judge. You do not want to listen if what they say is just evidence in their case. But you can listen if it is just to hear them.

"Mommy, Dante is such a liar. He is. And you always believe him. But he lies all the time."

Listening here is obviously tricky. Where is the line between case pleading, where they want you to judge for them and against their sibling, where they want you to *do something*—praise them or yell at or punish their sibling—and just wanting you to hear?

I want her to hear how Dante lies all the time and gets me in trouble and she never sees it.

You can make neutral comments: "That sure makes you mad"; "You think he lies all the time"; "I hear you."

Maybe, just maybe, as with love and sympathy, they may accept.

"It does. He is. He's such a liar."

Usually, however, this is not enough. They want to plead their case so you will do something, get you on their side. And with any given child, you learn over time whether just listening will ever be enough to satisfy.

"But Grayson said he was going to do it, which was why I didn't do it when you asked me to. And then he lied and said he never said he was going to do it and you yelled at me again when it was Grayson who was lying because he did say he was going to do it. I don't understand why you yelled at me. It's not fair. You have to yell at Grayson. You have to."

I will listen, but only to a point.

What Happens if You Get Out of the Middle

My basic recommendation in this book—don't get in the middle when siblings bicker—works even if up until now you have been doing just the opposite. Initially, your children may not be happy with the change.

"Mom, what are you doing? You have to listen to me. You don't understand. Gilbert is making those slurping noises again, and he does it just to bother me."

"Gosh, that must be really annoying."

"Mom, what are you doing? You don't understand. You have to do something. Talk to him. Gilbert, Mom wants to talk to you."

But little by little they will get the message.

Mom's gone crazy. She doesn't listen to me anymore. She lets Gilbert get away with everything. I'm going to have to deal with him myself.

Gradually, they learn that you are now a nonparticipant in their battles. Not only do you refuse to get involved, but as a result they come to you less often.

What's the point? All she says is stupid stuff, and she never listens.

If you do get out of the middle, you will find yourself staying out of the middle because it is so much more pleasant.

2.
The Nature of Sibling Relationships

Many questions can be raised about the rules I've presented for sibling bickering. If parents never get involved in their children's disagreements, how do kids learn about fairness? How do they learn healthy ways of negotiating? And if parents only separate the children but take no sides except when there is threat of physical harm, what is to prevent the older, bigger ones from regularly bullying—physically and verbally—the younger, smaller, more emotionally vulnerable ones? These are all real and valid concerns, and I have answers. First, however, I want to talk about the nature of sibling relationships—what their behavior toward each other does and does not mean. Let me start at the beginning.

In the Beginning

Soldiers going into a German concentration camp at the end of World War II found a group of six three-year-old orphans (three boys, three girls). As best as they could tell, these six children had their basic physical needs supplied by the adults in charge of them, but that was the extent of the care they received. Otherwise they had been left on their own. They were subsequently brought to England to live together in a special setting, where their behavior was described by the psychologist Anna Freud. She observed that the children ". . . cared greatly for each other . . . [they had] no wish other than to be together . . . were extremely considerate of each other's feelings." They would not even eat unless they made sure that the other children ate, and they did not like to be separated. Obviously they were very attached to each other.*

A simple fact is that from an early age children develop strong attachments to those other people in their lives with whom they have regular contact and who pay attention to them. It is in the nature of humans. Be in a child's life, give attention, and the child will love you. This very definitely applies to siblings.

---

* Anna Freud in collaboration with Sophie Dann, *The Psychoanalytic Study of the Child,* Volume VI (New York: International Universities Press, Inc., 1951), pp. 127–168.

—A Starbucks story—

A four-year-old boy and his two-and-a-half-year-old sister were with their father in a Starbucks, waiting for their order. Their father stood watching but not interacting with the two children. As they kept waiting, the boy did a stylized kind of walking, which his sister imitated. The boy, seeing her imitate him, then did a different kind of walk, and watched his sister who again tried to imitate his moves. He grabbed his sister by the arm, not roughly, and began pulling her along with him.

"Daddy, he's pulling me," said the girl quite happily. The boy was also smiling. Shortly afterward they left, and the two ran to the door next to each other. They clearly were enjoying each other's company.

—Another Starbucks story—

Two brothers, seven and five (I asked), were getting ready to leave. As the seven-year-old put on his snow pants, he started being silly—making faces, doing comic postures. His younger brother watched, giggling at the older boy's antics. The seven-year-old kept up his silly routine, clearly enjoying his highly responsive audience. When they both finally got their snowsuits on, the five-year-old went over and playfully poked his brother. His brother returned the poke. Both were definitely friendly and playful, not aggressive. They were enjoying each other.

Here are two fictitious stories that easily could be true.

Hugh had been throwing a miniature football to himself, trying to make acrobatic catches. He accidentally bumped into a table, knocking a glass vase onto the floor, breaking it.

Later that day Hugh's father noticed the glass fragments in the living room wastebasket.

"How did this happen?" he barked at his sons, who were in the room.

"Maggie"—the family cat—"did it," immediately responded Bruno, Hugh's older brother, jumping unasked to his brother's defense.

"We're making a surprise for you, Dad," laughed the three kids, running into and swiftly exiting the room where their father sat doing a crossword puzzle. Giggling and happy, animated talking could be heard from the kitchen.

"You're really gonna like it," said the kids with another flying visit to their father.

Finally, all three marched into the living room, Rocky carrying a plate covered with a dish towel. They were still laughing.

"It's your favorite." Now all of them were laughing hard. Rocky placed the plate on the table in front of their father.

"See what it is." More laughing.

Their father removed the dish towel to discover a plate with six vanilla cookies, each carefully "iced" with ketchup.

"See, ketchup-covered cookies." And the three burst into hysterical laughter.

Siblings often exhibit a flat-out enjoyment of and fondness for each other. They can be good audiences. They can be sources of admiration: "Jamie can make belching noises whenever he wants." They can be sharers of humor (which often does not seem so funny to adults). They can be allies. They can be buddies always available to play with. Or they can just be a warm body to lean against while watching TV. And all of this interaction and affection can belong to a realm wholly separate from parent involvement. Watching siblings engaged with each other, their happy back-and-forth, can be one of the true joys of parenting.

It does not take much. A normal part of being a child is that you develop a fondness for and an attachment to your siblings. Siblings can be a source of real pleasure in childhood. But as you know, it gets a little more complicated.

Here's Baby Jeannie

Three-year-old Buster watched in awe as his parents came through the front door carrying a tiny baby thing.

"Here's Baby Jeannie, your new sister."

From the start, Buster was very respectful of Baby Jeannie. He would kiss her and hug her very gently. He proudly told whoever would listen that he had a new baby sister.

"I have a new baby sister, and her name is Baby Jeannie."

Buster would say how he loved his new sister. "I love Baby Jeannie."

About two months after Baby Jeannie first joined the family, Buster's parents noticed that Buster, who had for many months been fully potty trained, was now regularly soiling his underpants. Also, there were more and more occasions where Buster, not normally a tantrum thrower, was having tantrums over nothing.

"I want Fruit Puffies."

"I'm sorry, sweetheart, I told you we don't have any."

"Go to the store."

"No, I'm not going to run out to the store right now just to get you Fruit Puffies."

And then Buster would have a tantrum.

What was his problem? The answer is obvious.

Buster does love Baby Jeannie. There is a good, loving part of Buster that genuinely cares about his baby sister, that gradually makes a real attachment to her. Buster is also very protective of Baby Jeannie.

"Mommy, will Rusty"—his aunt's dog, who sometimes visits the house—"hurt Baby Jeannie? We have to be careful."

But also, Buster is not happy about Baby Jeannie's arrival at all.

Before Baby Jeannie was here, I got all the attention. Now I get only some of it. I don't want to share it. For example, right now I'm here and they're not paying attention to me. They're paying attention to Baby Jeannie. This is not acceptable.

Buster loves Baby Jeannie, but he also very much minds her existence. It is called ambivalence. Both feelings exist side by side in the same body. Sometimes one rules, sometimes the other.

What to do?

You want to recognize for Buster his not-so-nice feelings about his sister's arrival and let him know that they are okay.

"I think sometimes you get mad because we pay attention to Baby Jeannie and not to you. It's okay to feel that way. Every kid with a new baby does."

You want to say that it's okay to be mad about Baby Jeannie. You may or may not be able to get this across, especially with very young children. Yet getting them to understand the normality of their jealous feelings is not what is most important. Far more important, far more eloquent and useful than anything you might say or try to explain, is that with the appearance of a new sibling you make sure to spend separate special and significant one-on-one time with the older sibling.

Baby Jeannie is here, but I still get special nice time with Mommy and Daddy, just like I used to. Baby Jeannie can't take that away from me. Of course, I would prefer that I get all the special time.

What matters is that they see that they still are special and still will get real time with you—though certainly not as much as before. What matters less is that you work through for them their jealous feelings. This is less important because regardless, there is nothing you can do to resolve the major problem, a problem that is not going to go away. A new sibling has come into the family, and that new sibling is not going anywhere.

"When does Baby Jeannie go back to the hospital?"

"Never. Baby Jeannie is going to be with us always."

"I want you to give her back."

"But you said you loved Baby Jeannie."

"I did. But now I'm finished. So it's time for her to go back."

There will also be good times, times when Buster enjoys his sister, when he sees her as part of his family and feels good about that, when he enjoys her presence. You get both—happy together, not at all so happy together.

What happens is that over time Buster does not exactly resolve his ambivalent feelings. The ambivalence remains. He just learns to live with it.

Baby Stands Up

Babies are cute. They sleep, smile, make little noises, and sometimes cry. Then they get older and bigger, and they learn to do more stuff.

Nida was her parents' first child. She was really cute, and her parents loved her to pieces. There couldn't have been a cuter child than Nida. She just kept on doing incredibly cute things. And good-natured?

"Little Miss Sunshine," her parents were fond of calling her. And gentle. Loving. Then, when Nida was a few months past her second birthday, Nida's family had a new addition. Nida now had a baby brother, Eugene. From the start, Nida loved Eugene. He was so cute. And Nida, true to her nature, was very loving and gentle with him.

"Good baby," she would say and gently pat his forehead. It is true that, similar to the story of Buster and Baby Jeannie, not long after Eugene's arrival Nida began showing a rather more temperamental side—having fits when she was not getting her way, seeming to get upset more easily over little stuff. But she was still Nida: incredibly cute, and, now that she was much more verbal, saying all kinds of incredibly cute things.

When Eugene was exactly ten months old, for the first time he pulled himself up to a standing position. His parents were delighted.

"Look, Eugene's standing!" exclaimed an equally delighted Nida.

But almost right away, a funny thing began to happen, especially if momentarily Nida and Eugene's parents were not watching. When Eugene would stand up, Nida would push him down. Quite regularly.

"No, Nida, you can't push down Eugene. He might get hurt."

"No, Nida, it's not nice to push down Eugene."

But try as they might—stern talks, time-outs, even temporary removal of certain favorite toys—Nida's parents did not seem able to cure Nida of her predilection for pushing down her brother whenever he stood up.

"Why do you do it?" Nida's parents would ask.

"Baby was bad," was Nida's most frequent explanation, although she never came up with the specifics as to what were her brother's crimes.

Usually, however, Nida would say, "I didn't do it," or "Baby fell," even when her parents had been looking directly at her and her brother when she had pushed him.

But then, even as her parents were thinking that they would always have to keep the siblings apart, Nida stopped doing it.

This is not an uncommon story.

My point: Nida was not an evil child. Her parents were doing nothing wrong. Nida's behavior toward her brother was not caused by any unusual or specific circumstances. There just was something about Eugene's standing up that particularly irked her. What?

He was getting special attention for it. "Isn't he wonderful?"

Push! *Well now, he's not quite so wonderful, is he?*

But also, in standing up, Eugene was moving out of the lower lying and crawling dimension of babies and was daring to intrude into the previously exclusive Nida domain of verticality.

An inevitable part of having a sibling is that you feel that certain space is yours alone, and his or her presence—just being—intrudes on that.

What to do?

Mainly, with very young children, you simply want to make very sure that they cannot hurt their new sibling. Always be there when a young child and baby are together. This is a necessary protection for the baby, and it is a psychological protection for the older child as well.

I have these terrible angry feelings toward my baby brother Eugene, but it doesn't matter because Mommy and Daddy are always there and will always stop me if I start to do anything that might hurt Eugene. My angry feelings are not scary because Mommy and Daddy will always be there to make sure nothing bad happens.

With the very young, you do *not at all* want to rely on your words, or their understanding, as a stay on their behavior.

You do want to explain. "No, you cannot hit your brother with a block. Blocks are hard and they can hurt him badly."

But these words are not controls, current protection for the baby; they are investments for the future, when the child's controls get better. For now you want her to understand, but it is your responsibility, not hers, that no harm befalls her baby brother. As mentioned, I am not sure I want to fall over backward trying to resolve jealous feelings. The new arrival is not going anywhere. Nor will sometimes not-loving feelings somehow just work themselves through. So long as there are more than one sharing the stage, the jealousy is there. It comes as part of the package.

"Hello. This is Mrs. Wilson. I understand you have an emergency foster child pickup service. There is a child for pickup here. Her name is Edna. She may fight you, so be prepared with some kind of sedation."

"You sound very young to be a mother."

"Um, I have a cold."

It is a dilemma. *It used to be just me and now it's not.* But it's more than that. It's more than the problem of Baby Eugene or Baby Jeannie. It is the loss of Paradise. As children get older, they find that the world is not perfect. Not only do Mommy and Daddy no longer seem to be under their total control, but the world out there, which becomes more and more important to them, is not under their control at all.

The solution to early sibling rivalry is not to work through all these feelings. They are part of that larger issue that never gets fully resolved: Not everything in life is as you want it.

Parents need to keep focused on the bigger picture.

Do your children get continuing real attention and love from you?

Are your children regularly exposed to all the richness that exists out there in the world separate from anything to do with Mommy's and Daddy's love and attention?

Are your children less than 100 percent successful at being the absolute ruler of you?

If all the answers are yes, then the odds are excellent that things will work out. In time, your children will gradually come to terms—sort of—with the major problem for us all: Life does not go exactly as we want it. Indeed, far from exactly.

The Baby Self and the Mature Self

With siblings there is love and there is something other than love. Yet there is one outstanding fact that more than any other determines why siblings act as they do toward each other. This basic fact of child and human psychology, more than any other, explains sibling behavior and what that behavior means in regard to their overall relationship.

Every day seven-year-old Steven comes home from school, takes off his jacket, and drops it on the floor. His hand when he drops the jacket is inches from a coat hook that is conveniently placed in the hallway for him to hang his jacket. Every day this happens. Without exception.

"Steven, how many times do I have to tell you to hang up your coat?"

Whatever the number, apparently it is not enough.

Steven is in second grade. Every day when he arrives at his school he goes to his cubby and, without anybody saying anything to him, he neatly hangs his jacket on a coat hook in his cubby. Every day. Without exception.

Not all second-graders are so good about hanging their jackets in their cubby. But many are, and yet they just as regularly never hang them up at home.

Justin's father arrives to pick up his son from his friend Damian's house.

"Dad, can we go to McDonald's?"

"No, I'm sorry, buddy, we don't have enough time."

"But you said we could go to McDonald's."

"No, I didn't say we could go. I said we might be able to go to McDonald's."

"But you promised."

"I didn't promise."

"Yes, you did. You promised. You promised. You always do this. I can't believe you're doing this again. You promised. You have to." At this point Justin is close to tears as he screams at his father.

"I don't understand," comments Damian's mother. "He was so well behaved until you got here."

Known to all parents yet somehow not recognized as a basic fact of human existence is that we all—kids and adults—have two distinct and separate modes of operating, really two distinct selves. One is an at-home and with-immediate-family version of us that just wants to relax, to unwind, to be nurtured, wants what it wants now, has minimal self-control, and will tolerate zero stress. It is the regressed version of our kids and of us. I call it the baby self. But there is another side that operates at a completely different and higher level of functioning. It is the part of us and our kids that goes out into the world, has patience, has self-control, is willing to delay gratification in order to work toward a goal, and can and will tolerate stress. I call this the mature self.

The baby self and the mature self operate in the course of a day very much like a shifting of gears. Both are us. Both are necessary. Baby selves are good. It is only in the baby self mode that we, that our kids, get the basic deep nurturing necessary for the development and maintenance of psychological health. I picture it like a boxer who goes out into the ring, fights, but then between rounds comes back into his corner, collapses, soaks up nurturing, and then, reinvigorated, heads back out into the ring. We need it, our kids need it—only our kids, being younger, need more of it.

Baby selves are good. They are warm, cuddly, affectionate. But it is in the nature of baby selves—it is part of the package—that when they aren't getting their way, baby selves can be rather less than cute and cuddly.

Another basic fact about baby selves is that home and parent bring out the baby self in a child. Just the presence of a parent, just the fact of being home, automatically causes the baby self to come out. This is significant in regard to sibling relationships. For the vast majority of what goes on between siblings is between their baby selves—and the nature of what goes on is dictated by the rules of thought and behavior that pertain to baby selves.

Baby Selves at Home

An interview with a baby self named Aaron. This could be anybody's baby self; they all think in the same way.

"Who's that?"

"My little brother."

"Do you like him?"

"I dunno. What's he doing?"

"Nothing."

"You're sure he's not into my stuff?"

"No."

"In that case he's okay. But he can be a pest. What's he doing now?"

"He's going into the refrigerator."

"He is? He better not be going after any of the ChocoPops."

The baby self goes into kitchen.

"Andre, what are you doing?"

"I'm just getting myself a glass of milk."

"Let me watch."

We interview Andre.

"What do you think of your brother?"

"I knew he was going to fuss about the ChocoPops, so I pretended to be getting milk. I'll sneak in and get the ChocoPops another time."

"Do you like him?"

"I don't know. When he's nice to me I do."

In the context of home and parents, the nature of the relationship between siblings is very primitive. Home and family bring out the far more babyish side in a child. Hence, siblings at home and with their family are like very primitive entities living side by side whose only governing rules are:

I want what I want now and I have no tolerance whatso-ever for anything that gets in my way or for any unpleasant-ness. The center of my universe is my parents, whom I have no interest whatsoever in sharing. Also everything that goes on exists in the present. I have no responsibility, there are no consequences for anything that I do, and anything that I did in the past has no relevance to now.

In the World Out There

Separate from home and family, where the other, more mature side tends to come out, it is a different story.

Two teenage brothers, close in age—maybe they were non-identical twins—worked at a McDonald's where I often go to write. They were Russian, though they obviously had been in the United States for a while, because they spoke totally unaccented English. To each other, however, they usually spoke in Russian. They seemed to work similar shifts, as I typically saw both of them there at the same time. In what I saw of them, they had a very relaxed but obviously close relationship—joking, talking with each other, clearly seeming to enjoy each other's presence. I never saw them snap at each other or get angry. I have no idea what they were like with each other at home, but it is very hard to imagine that there, in the context of home and family, the two brothers were not far more combative. But they were not that way at all when they were together at their job. Away from home they seemed obviously close, fond of each other.

Out there in the world, totally separate from home and family, a very different kind of relationship can prevail.

Anya is always beating up her little brother when they are home. But at school she watches out for him. I don't get it.

———

A well-known phenomenon. Leonard and Kara are return-ing from their every-other-weekend visit with their father. As always, they were well behaved and respectful of each other during their time there. But even as they come through the door of their mother's home, the fighting begins.

"Leonard, that's mine. Give it to me."

"It's not yours."

"Mom, it is too mine."

It takes them until Monday night to calm down every time they stay at their father's.

At their father's they are not comfortable enough to al-low their baby self sides to come out; there they act more like guests, on their good behavior. But now back at their mother's, the twins immediately revert to their more primi-tive baby selves.

"I will not give it back to you. Nobody said it was yours."

"Mom! Mom! Leonard's not giving it back to me. Mom!"

In the context of home and family, what are my siblings to me? There in that place, my view is very utilitarian. If they are nice or fun, if I am in the mood, I'll like being with them. Otherwise, if they are in my way, I will push them aside.

But there is a whole other side to sibling relationships. *Out there in the world, separate from home and family, I feel a closeness, an attachment to them. With them I feel safe. It is us against the world—not just me by myself.*

And in the context of my life as a whole I feel a very strong bond. They are—whether I like it or not—a part of me. They have been so much a part of my most intimate life. It is a very strong and very special bond.

There is this whole other mature side to our kids, though we may rarely get to see it. Baby selves don't change or grow up over time. They are always the same, and they do not vary from person to person. But the mature self grows. As part of normal development, it gradually takes over more and more of day-to-day functioning. Ultimately it can—for the most part—control the where and when of the baby self. But even into adulthood the baby self is still there as a part of us, and still necessary. That is, our children grow up. As adults they still have a baby self side to them—now mainly seen by adult partners and their own kids—but they do mature.

For all the baby self behavior that parents invariably get at home, as part of normal psychological development children move past this and do go out into the world and become respectful, productive citizens—and respectful and nice toward you as well.

As long as you have been a nurturing parent, but also have been willing to set limits and make demands, this change does come as part of normal development (even while often seeming very much like a miracle). And it comes not because at the last minute of their childhood you finally whipped them into shape.

"Rachel, you graduate from high school in an hour. Are you going to behave? You just better. Do you hear me? Now tell me. Are you going to behave?"

"Oh, okay. I guess so."

"Thank the Lord. "

It comes because they move on to the next major developmental stage—adulthood.

But what does this say about the often heedless, self-centered, at times most unattractive baby self behavior that so dominates what goes on between siblings? The babyish behavior that you get at home and between siblings is not necessarily a reflection of how they are on the outside and, more important, who they will become—even how they will feel and act toward each other as adults. And since home and parent invariably bring out the baby self in children, what you almost exclusively get to witness among your children is babies acting babyishly toward each other.

"Can't you three grow up?"

"No. Not here, not now, not with you around."

"How about as a special treat on my birthday?"

"Okay . . . No. Not really. Sorry."

"Richard, I'll give you fifty dollars if you are nice to Tommy."

"Tommy, I love you. Here's a big kiss. Now give me the fifty dollars."

"Mom, Richard kissed me. Now I have his germs on my face."

When They Are Older

Eric: "As kids we fought all the time. I thought Cedric was a baby who could always wrap Mom and Dad around his little finger. When I think back to what it was like when we were growing up together, I really don't remember ever liking him. All I remember is him as a pest and as someone who could always get Mom and Dad in on his side. But now he's my best friend."

Cedric: "Mainly what I remember is that Eric always treated me like dirt. He'd never do anything with me and he was always mean to me. I just wanted him to like me, to be nice to me, to pay some attention to me. But all I remember is that he was always angry at me. So I just learned to fight back the best I could. But now he's my best friend."

I mentioned earlier how my sisters and I didn't get along as children, but as adults we are good friends. Once we got to high school, our bickering more or less ceased. This was not due to any emerging fondness, but because as teenagers we were each deeply into our own adolescent concerns, and because we then rarely did much together as a family. Also, each of us had access to a car, and we promptly got our licenses when we turned sixteen. We went off to college and didn't have a lot to do with each other.

But after college, a new relationship began to emerge. We seemed to be nice to each other, to be supportive, and very noticeably—and surprisingly—we found we enjoyed each other's company. I definitely liked both of my sisters, and I know they liked each other. At first glance, this was very odd. But it really isn't.

There is a phenomenon—not always true, certainly vulnerable to all kinds of complexities, but nonetheless reflective of an underlying truth: Adult sibling relationships lie in a wholly separate realm from what existed during childhood.

The difference is simple and straightforward. When growing up in a home with a sibling, everything that goes on is in the baby self realm, which is about having fun and getting as much good stuff as possible, especially getting the biggest possible amount of parents. Everything else is irrelevant. All other motives are nonexistent. Hence, when growing up, our feelings toward our siblings are part of an amoral realm whose singular guiding principle—*Getting as much good stuff as I can and making sure my sibling is not getting more good stuff than me*—very often puts you and your sibling in direct competition. But when we become adults, parents—the greatest prize in childhood—are no longer the basic source of security and emotional nurturing. As an adult, love and support from parents no longer have the power to nurture that they once did. It is very much as if the now adult children have undergone an internal change whereby the emotional nutrients that were in the milk of parent love no longer have the ability to nourish. Now the nourishment must come from elsewhere—from the world separate from home and family.

Picture a fountain that gave the most marvelous and nourishing liquid, but always in limited supply. The fountain is still there, but it dried up long ago. Now you can visit it with your sibling, reminisce of times past when the fountain was vibrant and alive and you used to try to kill each other to get at its magic waters. But it's all ancient history. Each of you now has your own separate adult fountain. In adulthood, siblings are no longer part of that closed system of home and parent. That system is gone, replaced by the world out there.

So, too, sibling relationships are transformed. They now are part of that world as well.

In adulthood, all that might have contributed to a good relationship among siblings has that effect. There is now in adult life this person with whom you had tremendous intimacy, someone who more than anyone else shares much of the same history, the same experiences, someone who truly knows more about you than almost anyone else. Siblings have a huge reservoir of shared experience. In adulthood, that bond strongly comes into play. But because you both are now part of the world out there, its rules are in effect. That is, if there are people in your adult world who treat you badly, you are not going to like them and are not going to want to have anything to do with them.

Hence, in adult life a sibling is someone to whom you automatically feel close, but if he or she treats you badly, or has turned into someone you genuinely do not like, the closeness is usually not enough.

"Sandra's a stuck-up bitch. All she does when I see her is talk about how everything she does is so great, and she criticizes and puts down everything that I tell her about my life. Who needs that?"

On the other hand, if an adult sibling is nice and fun to be with, you're going to like him or her and want to have continuing contact.

"Reeva is always upbeat and funny. I like talking with her because she always puts me in a good mood."

In adult life I will always have a bond with my siblings.

But I may not like them and may not want them to be part of my life. If they are nice, I will.

Even if children are constantly at each other's throats or coldly ignoring each other, chances are that as adults they will like each other and get along. Of course, some adult siblings don't like each other, and they wouldn't like each other if they were unrelated. This is because of who they have become, who they are as adults, but rarely because of who they were or what their relationship was when they were growing up together.

Parent Favoritism in Adult Life

As an adult, Graham had never done as well as his two siblings, AnnaLee and Mason. Graham kept switching from job to job, never making anywhere near the kind of money his adult siblings did. At thirty-two he had a wife and three children, and lived in an apartment that was too small for them all.

Graham, AnnaLee, and Mason's parents, who were in their midsixties and mildly well off, decided (not as a result of any request by Graham) to give him a substantial amount of money that would enable him to buy a house.

They told their other two children, "We are very proud of how well the two of you have done. But we feel badly for Graham, and since we can afford it, we want to help with a house for him, Germaine, and the kids."

AnnaLee and Mason were less than pleased. Later they compared notes.

"I don't see why Graham should be treated specially just because he hasn't been able to do as well as either of us. It doesn't seem fair. We both work hard, harder than he ever did," said AnnaLee.

"I can't believe it. It's the same *poor-Graham* shit that he has always done since we were kids. And Mom and Dad keep buying it," said Mason.

Previously both AnnaLee and Mason had actually been generous toward their brother, occasionally helping him when he hit especially hard times. But from then on, seeing Graham in his house—which was not nearly as nice as either of theirs, but still one he hadn't paid for himself—both siblings were noticeably more distant with their brother. There always remained an underlying resentment.

"Where's my little man?" Five-year-old Teddy squealed with delight and went running into his grandfather's arms. His mother, Amy, watched happily.

"Here's Malcolm, Dad," said Gwen, Amy's sister, pushing her usually more reluctant and often sullen-seeming six-year-old son in the direction of his grandfather. But always with such visits, the cousins' grandfather showed a clear preference from the more bubbly Teddy. And as always, Gwen suffered for her son.

It's not fair. Malcolm is his grandson, too. Just as much as Teddy.

Though in truth Amy had done nothing wrong, Gwen could not help feeling a certain resentment and coldness toward her sister as she thought of the less favored status of her son.

Money is the main issue that divides adult siblings. But grandchildren can be tricky, too. Unfortunately, good adult relationships between siblings can be damaged or even undone where parents, well meaning though they may be, act in a clearly unequal manner. The gains of maturity are not set in cement and can be set back if parents, especially in regard to money, do not treat their children equally.

Mother's End Table

For three years when they were growing up, a small oak end table had sat next to Darlene and Angela's mother's bed. But then it was moved to the attic because their mother wanted a table with more space on top. Thirty-five years later, their mother died.

Their mother's will was explicit and their inheritance had been divided up. Belongings of any value had been appraised and were split between the sisters based on equal distribution of appraised worth. The end table had been described as having no significant value.

"Darlene, I'd like that little oak end table. I've always liked it, and Mother said that I could have it when she died."

"Mother said what? When did she say that?" Darlene,

who had previously noticed but not cared at all about the table, suddenly discovered that she had a passionate need to own it herself. "Mother would never have said something like that without first asking me if it was okay."

"Well, she did."

"She wouldn't have."

After much bitter arguing that ended up involving lawyers, Angela got the end table. The sisters, who had been close friends throughout their adult lives, never spoke to each other again.

What was their problem? Wasn't their relationship, which had been a very important and positive part of their adult lives for the past thirty-five years, far more important than a stupid (and, frankly, ugly) end table that neither had even thought about during those same thirty-five years?

No, I never before understood how greedy and selfish Angela was. Now I do.

Darlene could never get over that Mother liked me better, which Mother did. I really don't need her aggravation as part of my life.

All children assume an unwritten birthright: *I get my full share of the love that my parents have to give. If I am one among siblings, then we all get exactly equal full shares.*

For example two sisters, Shannon and Shelly, growing up together. Shannon thinks: *My parents love me and Shelly the same. It may be that day to day I feel that she always gets her way and I don't, and she always gets the better stuff than me, but overall in the biggest picture, my parents do love me and Shelly the same. It's just that she's a whiny, weaselly conniver—which my parents never get to see—so that she always wins and I always lose.*

But overall, I know that my parents love me and Shelly the same.

This certainty that overall they get their fair share is very important because it is what keeps the mindless pigginess of the baby self at bay.

I want everything, but if I truly believe that I am getting my fair share, I do not have to get everything all of the time. Overall, I am satisfied.

The day-to-day world of specifics is another story.

Throughout the school day, Shannon does not worry at all about getting her fair share. But at home, when Shelly gets more gumdrops than her, she has a major fit. If it sees her sibling get even the slightest, tiniest bit more, her baby self will not, cannot let that pass.

In adult life we move on. Now our fairness deal is not with parents but with the world at large. Now we can be allies with our siblings, supportive of each other, not constantly having to fight over every crumb of parental favor. For the most part, we manage to deal with the cosmic unfairness of life. We make our overall peace. But it is a fragile peace, for the baby self in us never grows up. In our adult relationship with our siblings, we move past the baby self cravings that so dominated our childhoods together. But mature adult sibling relationships can be undone. They can be pulled back into their earlier primitive ways. Perhaps it should not be this way, perhaps we should all be above it, but it is in the nature of humans that we are all vulnerable.

Even as adults, if we see a chink in the fairness deal with our siblings, so long ago seemingly resolved, we are still vulnerable. It can all come flooding back.

What to do?

It is hard, because those forces inside us are strong. You want to try your best not to lose sight of the bigger adult-life picture.

I like Angela. I've liked her the whole time that we have been adults. She has been a very positive part of my life. I know I feel sick every time I see that end table at her house, but it's just a table. Having a sister is a lot more important than my feelings about a stupid table.

Try your best. But recognize that it is not easy.

3.

But What About?...

I have recommended very specific solutions to sibling bickering. These recommendations raise a number of legitimate questions. Let me answer what are, I think, the major questions raised.

How Do Children Learn About Fairness?

So if parents don't get involved, how do their children learn about fairness? How do they learn to negotiate in disagreements?

Let me first talk about fairness, but I'll divide it into two questions. First, how do children learn what is fair? And second, how do they come to believe in fairness, genuinely want to be fair in their dealings with others? You can know the rules but not want to follow them.

How do they learn about fairness?

Claudia divides up the jelly beans.

"Now we are going to fairly divide up the jelly beans. I get all the red ones and you get all the black ones."

"That's not fair. I hate the black ones."

"It is fair because I hate the black ones more than you do."

If left on their own, all they would know is that the biggest gets the best and the most.

How do they learn the rules of fairness? From you.

"Andrea, you got to lick the cookie batter from the bowl last time. Now it's Ryan's turn."

"You each get to pick out one of the regular-sized candy bars."

But really the rules of fairness are pretty simple.

Everybody is supposed to get the same amount of good stuff and the same amount of bad stuff.

Children learn the rules of fairness from you, but, regardless, they also learn them from their regular exposure to the rest of the world.

"Okay, boys and girls. We each get two cookies. No, Jonathan, you have to put those other cookies back. If you take that many there won't be enough cookies for everybody. It wouldn't be fair."

Learning about fairness comes with going out and gradually becoming part of the civilized world separate from home and family.

The truth, as any parent knows, is that children at a very early age do grasp and swiftly latch onto the concept of fairness.

"It's not fair!"

They get it and they get it early. But for their own purposes.

"It's not fair. Seven months ago, it was July seventeenth to be precise, you let Peter get candy when we were waiting in the supermarket line. And now you're saying I can't get candy. It's not fair."

The concept of fairness is a good thing. It is how children learn to act well. It becomes a foundation of their overall moral sense. But a problem is that once children get the concept, it also becomes the number one battering ram to be used with parents when they are not getting their way.

"It's not fair. Why can't I get a pony?"

But they do understand the fairness concept.

Everybody is supposed to get the same.

They know the rule, which makes the question of making sure that they learn about fairness not a major worry. The big issue isn't learning the fairness rules. The real issue is their willingness to be fair when they have to give up something.

So how do they become people who believe in fairness, genuinely want to be fair in their dealings with others?

They get that from you, but not from what you tell them. They get it if they see you trying to be fair. Not all the time about everything—as discussed, with the little stuff speed sometimes needs to take precedence—but certainly about important things.

Beverly and Rene got to fly out and stay with Grandma Williams, but we felt Gary was too young. Now that he is older, even though money is a little tighter, we want to make sure that he gets his chance to do the same.

Danny's room is much smaller than Elliott's, so we let Danny have a corner of the TV room that is his and where he can store some of his stuff.

Equally important, do you demonstrate fairness? Do they see you, in dealing with others, trying to be fair?—not just with them, your children, but with others, as well. Do they see you acting fairly or not? It is less about fairness in terms of exactly equal treatment and more about the human part that underlies fairness: Do you show your children that you genuinely care about people and their welfare?

Perhaps most important of all, you can present to them, try to instill in them, good values, good models of fairness, but their acceptance or rejection of these will come from their acceptance or rejection of the teacher, you. That is, if you have been a good, caring parent, then that package of who you are, what you stand for, becomes a part of them. If not, it doesn't.

Let me tell a story from my childhood, one that has stuck in my memory over the years.

My mother, my sisters, and I were walking in downtown Philadelphia. Ahead of us, lying on the sidewalk, was a raggedy man. People were walking by him paying little notice. But my mother, concerned that he might need help, sought out a policeman and said that there was a man lying on the sidewalk who looked like he needed help. I don't remember anything else of the incident.

The story is no big deal except that I remember it so clearly after all these years. It is the rule that she taught. You are supposed to try to help people, *all* people, even raggedy-looking men who are lying on the sidewalk.

It was not that one incident that taught me my mother's moral beliefs. But the fact that it stayed with me all the years says that it was a pretty accurate encapsulation of what she stood for. How did I learn her moral system? Not from that incident, but from the repeated but long-forgotten instances of what she did day to day.

The point is, I had a nice mother. I felt that I did get from her that special unconditional love so treasured by all children. And as a direct result, my overwhelming sense of my mother was that she was good. Good to me. And so—though I may not always live up to it—I got from her as part of me: *It's good to care about everybody.*

Where do children learn about fairness? From you. Not from how you fairly try to orchestrate their arguments with siblings, but above all from your own charity toward others and from your love of them.

How Do Children Learn to Negotiate?

If left to solve disputes on their own, how do siblings learn to negotiate disagreements?

Let me tell a made-up but possible story.

—*Version 1*—

Simon, ten, Mikhaila, nine, and Dominick, six, were playing Wiffle ball outside behind their house. Their father was reclining in a deck chair enjoying the sun.

The game was that Simon and Mikhaila would pitch to each other and Dominick would run around collecting the batted balls that the pitcher was unable to field.

"I want to bat," complained Dominick.

"No, Dominick, you're no good at hitting. It's too boring if you bat," said Simon.

"Then I want to pitch."

"No way. You can't throw it right. You have to be the fielder," said Mikhaila.

"But I want to bat."

"Well, you can't, because you're not good enough."

"Daddy, they won't let me bat."

At this point their father, who had been watching, intervened.

"Mikhaila and Simon, if you're going to play, you have to let Dominick bat and pitch. I know he isn't as good as you two, but you must let him have chances, too. He doesn't have to get as much time batting and pitching as either of you, but he has to get his chances."

"But he can't bat and he can't pitch and it's boring and if he does it's stupid and it's no fun."

"You'll just have to put up with it. Dominick has to get his chances, too."

The children continued their Wiffle ball game, but now with occasional turns for Dominick batting and pitching.

—Version 2—

The same story, but in this version their father was sitting in the kitchen talking with his brother who had stopped over. He could see his children but could hear little through the closed window.

The scene went as before.

"You have to be the fielder."

"But I want to bat."

"Well, you can't, because you're not good enough."

In this version, however, with Dominick's father inside and less immediately available, Dominick did not pursue that option.

"It's not fair. I want to bat."

"Well, you can't."

Grumbling, Dominick resumed fielding, but then after a little while—both bored with his limited role and mad that he was not given a turn—he decided to quit.

"I'm not playing anymore unless I bat." He walked over to the swings and began playing there.

"Who needs you, little baby."

Simon and Mikhaila continued playing. Soon, however, they found that without Dominick to retrieve the batted balls, their play didn't go as well, wasn't as much fun.

"Do you want to let him bat?" asked Simon.

"I guess," said Mikhaila. "But let's not give him long turns."

"Okay, Dominick, you can bat."

"I want to pitch, too."

"All right, but you can't have long turns."

The children then continued their Wiffle ball game, now with occasional turns for Dominick both batting and pitching.

Obviously, siblings do not always work out compromise solutions. A possible ending might have been Dominick storming off and not playing anymore because he was too mad or because his brother and sister were unwilling to concede anything to him, even though it meant that they had to chase the balls. But this, too, would have been a resolution—perhaps not as desirable, but a resolution nonetheless.

"I hate them. They don't want me. I'll play by myself."

"It sucks having to chase the balls, but it is better than letting him bat and pitch."

Going back to the first version where their father intervened, that, too, might have had a different ending. The children might not have so easily accepted their father's imposed resolution.

"You'll just have to put up with it. Dominick has to get his chances, too."

"No! No way! You don't understand. It'll ruin everything. He doesn't know how to play at all."

"I do too."

"Dad, it's not fair. He just comes to you and gets what he wants. It's not fair. It will ruin our game."

"Yeah, you always favor him. We're never going to include you, Dominick, because you ruin everything. You little baby, you always run to Daddy."

"Dad, they say they are not going to include me, and they called me a baby."

"That's it, the three of you, go to your rooms and I don't want any of you coming out until November."

So how do children learn to solve disputes? The answer is that by being left on their own, time and again they learn to negotiate. These are real negotiations, where children are being asked to give up something, where feelings come in. By being left on their own and only by being left on their own do they get repeated practice at real negotiation. You can be told what to do, but you learn by doing.

Here is the real basis of negotiation:

What am I willing to give up? What is not negotiable? What, even though it's not my preference, can I live with? How can we negotiate without getting so angry that they or I might leave, ending the negotiating—but also ending whatever it was we were doing? Or maybe the arguing becomes too loud or physical, such that our parent will intervene to separate us, again ending the negotiation and our mutual activity.

This is what real sibling negotiation is about.

The parents' role that I recommend in regard to disagreements gives each sibling the following message:

If a disagreement gets so noisy—for whatever reason— that it disturbs our parents, they will come and separate us.

I can always use them for protection from getting hurt. I can either run to them, "Fred's going to hit me," or scream real loud, "Eeeee!" so that they will come and separate us, ending the possibility of me getting hurt.

That is, they have to somehow work it out, trying to stay within the limits that won't cause the process to break down. But if it does break down, there is always a safety net to prevent serious damage.

Rough Justice

The following are two real-life situations I observed. The first is real but is made up of two separate incidents that I have lumped together as one; the events nonetheless represent what actually went on. The second is as I witnessed it.

—Story 1—

A nine-year-old girl, her seven-year-old brother, and an unrelated seven-year-old girl were playing foosball (table soccer) beside a swimming pool. There were many adults sitting around the pool. I had no idea which were the parents of the children involved, for during the time that I watched, there was no interaction between any of the adults and any of the children.

The nine-year-old girl took charge. "I'll be the captain and you'll be my assistant," she said to the younger girl. "You'll be the helper," she added to her brother.

"I don't want to be the helper."

"But that's the way the game is played."

This seemed to be the first time any of them had confronted foosball, so they were all on equal footing as to how the game was supposed to be played. The boy glowered briefly but then allowed his sister to continue the game.

They began a stylized game involving occasional turning of the handles to move the soccer players, placing the small metal ball in front of the players, and occasional kicks—a game that had nothing to do with real foosball, clearly a game that the nine-year-old girl was making up on the spot. It was basically a role-playing game as designed by the girl. They played for a little while.

"When do I get a turn?" said her brother.

"When I say so," the girl said. "I'm the captain."

"I want to be the captain," said the boy.

"You can't, because I'm already the captain," said the girl.

The boy stalked off.

"Don't be a baby," said the girl.

"You're a baby," said the boy.

"Fine, we'll play without you."

She and the other girl continued playing. The boy stood off to the side for a while watching and kicking at pebbles outside the cemented area of the pool. After a few minutes—no more—he moved back to standing at the foosball table. He said nothing, but his sister without missing a beat included him back in the game.

"Now you're the other soldier, but you don't like this one."

"I want to be the captain," said the boy, swiftly grabbing the metal ball and running about twenty feet away and then turning, defiantly looking at his sister.

"You're such a baby. Give us back the ball."

The boy just stood.

"Fine, you can't be the captain, but you can be the captain soldier. That means you can turn the men, but only when I say so."

The boy stood some more.

"The captain soldier is very important," said the girl.

The boy shrugged and moved back to his sister, handing her the ball.

The older girl was skilled. She had a good imagination. She was able to keep the game going for a good period of time. They played, mainly her giving orders and telling the story for maybe fifteen or twenty minutes. They then abandoned the game and went back into the pool.

—Story 2—

A fourteen-year-old girl and her twelve-year-old brother were standing in line at McDonald's. Their parents were off to the side engaged in a discussion with another couple, not paying attention to the two children.

The boy kicked the girl in the leg. The girl kicked him. The boy kicked her back. The girl again returned the kick. These were basically back-side-of-the-foot karate-style kicks—not very hard, but hard enough to hurt. Each had a look that was half smile, half determination. The boy kicked again. So did the girl. The exchange went on for maybe a total of five kicks, with each perhaps getting slightly harder. The parents still seemed to pay no attention to what was going on.

It was then the family's turn to give their order, and the kicking ended. Watching the back-and-forth, I expected that at any moment the situation would escalate into a real fight or at least some kind of genuinely angry confrontation. It never happened. I can only say that watching the (sort of) fight, my sense was that the brother and sister were each getting a little angrier with each kick, clearly moving in a direction that was going to end up in some kind of out-of-control, angry fight. As I said, it never happened. The sort-of fight just stopped and they moved on to whatever was next.

For the rest of time that the brother and sister were in McDonald's, they seemed to be getting along fine, very much as if the kicking exchange and the angry feelings it must have engendered had never happened. The parents seemed to be wholly oblivious to what had gone on between their two children.

My only point with Story 1: What would have happened if a parent had intervened? I can imagine only a less pleasant, less swiftly resolved outcome.

My only point with Story 2: Clearly, I was witnessing the end product of a long history between brother and sister in which they long ago had precisely worked out limits of aggression that would not escalate—make either of them too mad—or bring in parent intervention.

An overwhelming fact about sibling fighting, a fact from which I do not back down, is that the presence of a parent in a sibling disagreement immediately and inevitably brings out in all children involved the infinitely piggy, regressed, all-it-cares-about-is-getting-as-much-as-possible-of-the-parent side of a child. And along with that, the concomitant abandonment of any interest whatsoever in resolutions other than totally getting one's way.

Why would the injection of parents ever be desirable in response to sibling bickering? If there is no parent intervention, how do children learn the skills of negotiation? By actually doing it—again and again.

Older Bullying the Younger

If all you do with sibling fighting is intervene to stop it if it is bothering you, and come down on one side or the other only when there is threat of harm, what is to stop an older sibling from regularly bullying and putting down a younger brother or sister?

Let me first address bullying.

What is to stop ten-year-old Anthony from regularly bullying his seven-year-old brother Philip, hitting him whenever he feels like it, physically bullying and intimidating him in order to get his way, or maybe just beating him up because he feels like it?

The truth is, if they are two typical brothers, sometimes Anthony probably will.

"Mom, Anthony is twisting my arm."

"Shut up, you little baby."

"Mom, Anthony is twisting my arm."

"The two of you, stop it right now."

"But Anthony was twisting my arm."

"If you can't be together without fighting, you'll both have to go your rooms."

If this is all that happens, what's to stop Anthony, if he feels like it, from regularly pummeling his younger brother?

There are a number of strong and important controls.

You do intervene, you do take sides—whenever there is threat of harm. The message to Anthony: *Under no circumstances may you ever cause harm to your brother.*

If you do not like what is going on—bullying—you can always intervene to stop it, by separating the children.

As mentioned, if a child is truly not enjoying what is going on with a sibling, he can either run to you or scream loudly enough that you will intervene. Either way, the unpleasant—for him—interaction is brought to a halt.

Unless there is threat of harm, you do not want to come down unilaterally against Anthony. If you follow this policy, there is a last very significant control on Anthony's aggression toward Philip. If parental favor, taking sides (other than where there is threat of harm), is truly removed, never enters into their conflicts, then so too is removed any deep reason for Anthony to dislike his brother.

If part of Anthony's childhood is not, "Mommy, Anthony hit me," resulting in, "Anthony, you come here this minute"; if there is no Philip running to a parent with Anthony getting in subsequent trouble; if that scene is simply not part of their childhoods; if Anthony sees that Philip's being younger, smaller, and weaker cannot automatically bring a parent in on Philip's side, then the number one reason for older disliking younger is removed.

Philip may pester Anthony, get in his space when he does not want him there. Philip may sometimes get into or wreck Anthony's stuff. But these are all of-the-moment annoyances, not causes of deep resentment. I cannot emphasize this strongly enough. Over the years in talking to child clients about themselves and younger siblings, where there was real resentment, the one invariable complaint was the ability of their younger sibling to get their parents on his or her side. If this does not happen with Anthony and Philip, then the greatest single impediment to Anthony actually liking his younger brother is removed. Anthony won't like Philip all the time. At times Anthony will find his younger brother a pest. At times Anthony will use his superior size to take advantage of Philip—he will even feel good about it. But there will also be times that Anthony will like his younger brother, will actually be nice to him.

Anthony will at times bully Philip because he is bigger and can do it. But *not* always intervening against Anthony when he acts aggressively toward his younger brother, *not* taking sides, more than anything else you might do does control and reduce—though not eliminate—the amount of bullying that will go on.

———

But regardless of how much, isn't Philip damaged by the even occasional bullying?

An overwhelming fact is that younger siblings, if the older are even the slightest bit nice to them, invariably like, look up to, even idolize their older sibling. The little ones hate it when they get picked on by their bigger sibling, do at the time suffer, but this does not seem to get in the way of at other times—when the older siblings are actually nice to them—loving their older sibling. And of course those being-nice times can be dramatically increased where the Anthonys of the world do not have a permanent grudge against their younger brothers.

Philip can always get them on his side because he is such a baby.

A common scene is a younger sibling, only minutes before in tears as a victim of older sibling nastiness, now, that left behind, right back trying to engage the older sibling.

"Anthony, will you play with me?"

And maybe Anthony, because he was just mean to Philip and currently has no grievance against him, will be more disposed to say, "Yeah, I guess so. What do you want to do?"

Verbal Abuse

What about verbal abuse? Children can be amazingly cruel. Doesn't that damage the younger one's self-esteem?

"Ivanna, look what I did," said six-year-old Caleb, proudly

showing the drawing that he had just finished to his ten-year-old sister. "See, it's a horse and that's me riding it."

"That doesn't look like anything. That's a baby drawing," said Ivanna. "You don't know how to do anything."

Caleb started to cry.

"You are such a baby," said Ivanna, and walked out of the room.

Caleb, still crying, went to his mother. "Ivanna says I'm stupid and I can't draw."

"You're not stupid, sweetheart."

"I am. I draw like a baby. Ivanna says so."

"Let *me* see your drawing."

"No, Ivanna says it's ugly."

The children's mother went looking for Ivanna. She found her in her room.

"Ivanna!"

"What?"

"What did you say to your brother?"

"I didn't say anything."

"Why do you always have to put him down? He's six years old. What you say to him really hurts his feelings."

"But Mom, he's just a big baby. All he does is cry all the time."

"You cried a lot when you were his age."

"Not as much as him, I didn't."

"I don't care, Ivanna. You cannot put him down like you do. You are older and bigger and you cannot talk to him like that."

This is the issue about which parents seem to feel the strongest—the one that makes it hardest for them to remain uninvolved.

You don't understand. Caleb is the kindest, gentlest, sweetest, most sensitive little boy in the world. He is so generous and so open and it just breaks my heart when Ivanna puts him down like she does. It breaks my heart.

Let me talk briefly about one common parent intervention—the lecture.

Ten-year-old Michael regularly made cutting comments to his five-year-old brother Todd.

"Michael, turn off the computer, I want to talk to you."

"Mom, I'm *really* in the middle of something."

"Turn it off."

"This is about Todd, isn't it?"

"Yes, it is."

"Mom!"

"Todd is five years old. He's just a little kid. I know he can be a pest, but that's what five-year-olds do. You have to cut him some slack. He doesn't mean anything by what he does. He doesn't always understand that he's being a pest. He doesn't know any better. You can't always be yelling at him and putting him down like you do.

"He looks up to you. You are more than five years older than him. You have to be the one who is more mature. I know that you are capable of it. It's just not fair to Todd."

"Mom, he's a little brat and he does know what he's doing."

"No, Michael, he's five years old. You have to try harder. You have to be more tolerant. He's just a little kid. And really, he does look up to you."

This is a good lecture: calling on a child's maturity, expecting a higher standard of behavior from him, making him understand that younger siblings come from a completely different place and cannot be held to the same standards of behavior. The only problem with this talk—which you probably know well—is that it does not work at all, not even a little bit. If it did work, I would be for it. In fact, maybe you should do it anyway. It is a good thing to say. It's true that older children should be more mature. They should understand that their younger sibling, like it or not, does operate at a less mature level than they because their younger sibling *is* less mature.

But the talk has a downside, and there is no way around it. The talk breeds resentment.

That little baby. Mom doesn't understand. I'm the one who gets in trouble. He's the one who acts like a little jerk. Why should I always get the lecture for what he does? They should be thanking me. I should get extra allowance for how much I put up with him. But Mom doesn't understand. I could be a lot worse. I do cut him slack. A lot. But the only thing that happens is that I get yelled at anyway.

The lecture *feels* right. As I said, I'm not against it; maybe these things need to be said. But don't expect it to work.

Between Baby Selves

Let's get back to the question: Don't the constant put-downs affect the overall self-esteem of the younger victim?

As discussed, interaction between siblings exists in a special realm, the realm of the baby self. In regard to what you think about yourself, your self-esteem—*Am I smart, am I stupid? Am I good looking, am I ugly? Am I strong, am I weak? Am I cool, am I nerdy?*—in the realm of the baby self, none of this applies. It is the realm where siblings interact with siblings. It makes no logical sense, but it is an absolute fact nonetheless, that for siblings, what goes on in their world when they interact with each other does not count.

Here's another made-up but could-be-true story.

Holly was a truly wonderful girl. Sensitive, independent of spirit, genuinely caring of others. One day at school she was with a couple of her friends when one of them spoke of a younger schoolmate who had a serious learning disability.

"He's such a retard," said Holly's friend.

Holly reacted immediately. "Jeannine, you should never call somebody a retard. It's not his fault."

"Well, look who's Miss Perfect."

But Holly stuck to her guns. "No, it's not right."

That evening Holly related the incident to her mother. Holly was shocked that one of her friends would actually talk about a kid as a "retard."

"I can't believe Jeannine said that," Holly said to her mother.

But wouldn't you know it, Holly happened to have a couple-of-years-younger brother, Garth, who had a serious learning disability and whom Holly called a retard all the time.

Holly's mother listened incredulously to her daughter's outrage.

"Excuse me."

"What?"

"You call Garth a retard all the time."

"But it's not the same."

That's my point. Anyone who has a sibling knows this is the way it is. What goes on among brothers and sisters—as opposed to similar interactions with the world separate from family—*really is not the same.* Within the family, in the realm of the baby self, it is not the same, it does not count. Holly is stating what we all intuitively know to be a basic truth.

Suppose somebody else called Garth a retard. Holly might well jump to her brother's defense.

"Don't you dare talk that way about my brother."

But she can talk that way. It's not the same.

It's okay for me to call him a retard. But it's not okay if you call him a retard. I can call him a retard because he's my brother. It's not the same.

More important, it is not just Holly who perceives it differently. So does Garth. When his sister calls him a retard, it regularly infuriates him, drives him crazy, but really the put-down could be anything. Holly could call him a noodle, and if it was said in the same scornful tone, it would get just as big a response. She could call him anything so long as she did it in a sufficiently scornful manner. Garth gets upset not because he is sensitive about his learning disorder (which he probably is). His sister's taunt, as it happens in his baby self realm, is not about his self-esteem. Garth gets upset when his sister calls him a retard because he correctly perceives that she is intentionally trying to annoy him. It is no different from Holly licking her finger and then rubbing her saliva-wet finger on the victim's arm.

"Stop that. Stop that. That's gross. Mom, Holly put her saliva on my arm."

"Mom, Holly called me a retard."

If someone not a sibling, especially a peer at school, were to call him a retard, the effect would be totally different. Garth would worry that he really was retarded and as such different from and not acceptable to his peers. But his sister Holly calling him a retard doesn't say anything about that; it just drives him crazy. He knows the difference. Holly calling him a retard is not a statement of his worth by judges about whose opinion Garth desperately cares, but a tease by a sister intended to annoy, which it does but doesn't touch the self-esteem part of him. It is no different, no more relevant to issues of self-esteem, self-worth, than Holly saying, "Naah! Naah! Naah! Naah! Naah!" That level of personal meaning.

Think about Caleb, whose sister disparaged his drawing. Within the family, parents, not siblings, are the ultimate dispensers of value. Despite Caleb's apparent sensitivity to his older sister's criticism, his mother's encouraging words do win out.

"Mommy says my drawing is good."

"Well, it's not. It's a baby drawing."

"No, Mommy says it's good. She said for a six-year-old boy it's a very good drawing."

"Well, she doesn't know anything."

"She does too."

"No, it's baby drawing. And your lower lip is weird."

"Mommy, Ivanna said my lower lip is weird."

It is not that Ivanna's put-downs will not continue to upset Caleb. They always will. But she is not the dispenser of self-worth. Her put-downs do not speak to Caleb's self-esteem. They are in the realm of teasing, aggravating, crazy making, but not self-worth.

If you don't like the taunting, if you are uncomfortable with it, you can always stop it by separating taunter and taunted. *"I don't like the name calling and the put-downs so I'm going to separate the two of you whenever I hear them."* But there is a major benefit to not always too swiftly jumping in to protect the little one.

Counterpunching

Ivanna and Caleb—A Different Version

"Ivanna, look what I did. See, it's a horse and that's me riding it."

"That doesn't look like anything. That's a baby drawing."

This is not the first time that Ivanna has belittled something that Caleb's done. In fact, she usually has only negative things to say where Caleb is concerned. And in this version, Caleb has over time developed a rather different kind of response to his sister's put-downs.

"You never like anything I do."

"That's because everything you do is like a baby, which is what you are."

"*You're* a baby," says Caleb, picking up his drawing and heading into the other room. "Mommy will like it."

Caleb has learned to stand up for himself. He has learned the technique of counterpunching. It is a *very* useful skill to develop. Picture a boxer going out into the ring against an opponent—except this particular boxer keeps his hands in his pockets. It doesn't work so well.

Let me tell a story.

A man goes into a store. At the cash register he fumbles getting out his money. The clerk says, "Do you mind? There are people waiting."

97

The man immediately flushes in anger, humiliated. But he says nothing. Finally he gets out his money, pays, and leaves. But he fusses in his head about how rude the store clerk was. About what he might have said to the clerk but didn't. About how he always seems to come off as a wimp. Finally, after about half an hour of having uncomfortable feelings as a result of the incident, he lets it go.

A different man comes into the store. He, too, is slow getting out his money. The same clerk is rude to him. But this man does not keep silent.

"Take your time, why don't you?" the clerk says sarcastically.

"Excuse me, who do you think you are talking to? You don't talk to customers that way. Where's the manager? Maybe I won't talk to him this time because I'm in a hurry. But you better watch how you talk to customers or you won't have your job very long."

The man then gets out his money, pays, and leaves the store.

They really have some jerks working in stores these days. What's the world coming to, he thinks as he leaves. The man feels fine. Nor does he think about the incident any further.

A quick counterpunch deflects and insulates against verbal barbs. They more easily bounce off instead of hitting and sinking in. It takes out much of the sting. It is also called standing up for yourself.

Another Two-Version Story

—Version 1—

"Maisee, you are so stupid, and you smell."

Maisee's eyes started to well up with tears. Her lower lip quivered.

"Maisee, you are such a baby."

Now Maisee's tears flowed silently until she burst from the room running to her mother.

"What is it, sweetheart?"

"K-k-kayla says I'm stupid and I smell," sobbed Maisee.

—Version 2—

"Maisee, you are so stupid, and you smell."

"You're stupid and you smell."

"You're such a baby, Maisee."

"You're such a baby."

"Just repeating what I say doesn't make you not be a baby. You are still a baby."

"You're still a baby, and you have ugly toenails."

"That's so stupid, Maisee."

But actually, Maisee one day had randomly hit upon the toenail insult and, for whatever reason, it always upset Kayla, so Maisee, intuiting a winner, always came back to it.

"You have ugly toenails."

"Did I say you smell, Maisee? Because you do."

———

If Maisee were your child, which version would you prefer?

Learning to counterpunch occurs only when a parent does not get too much in the way of allowing it to happen.

Let's go back to the story of Caleb and Ivanna, who criticized her brother's drawing. Caleb went to his mother.

"Ivanna says my drawing is stupid."

"Gosh, I'm sorry. That must have made you feel bad."

"She always says I'm stupid. She does."

And Caleb started to sob.

"She does. I hate her. She says I'm stupid."

Caleb sobbed some more, whereupon his mother picked him up and held him. Caleb continued to sob.

"She says I'm stupid."

Let's say that this goes on for a while, ten or fifteen minutes, until Caleb is finally calmed down. And let's say that this happens virtually every time Caleb's sister puts him down. Caleb gets very upset. Goes to his mother. Stays upset. Gets a lot of love and sympathy. And each time it takes maybe ten or fifteen minutes of love and sympathy before Caleb calms down.

It so upsets Caleb when Ivanna teases him.

There is an important role that we play as parents: putting things in perspective. Caleb's mother wants to give Caleb comfort and sympathy. He does get upset when his sister teases him. His mother should give him comfort and sympathy—*to a point*. Because there's a very real risk that the love and sympathy that Caleb gets from being upset can become the end in itself.

Gosh, if I get upset whenever Ivanna teases me and I go to Mommy, Mommy always give me lots of love and attention.

This is seriously not good for a number of reasons.

When Caleb is teased by his sister, his aim can become to use his upsetness as a means of milking as much love and sympathy from his mother as he can. If so, he then has no investment—just the opposite—in trying to learn to deal with his sister on his own. So he won't.

Caleb can believe too much in his own misery. As he invests in being miserable, in order to sustain it, he must believe in it. His misery can take on a life of its own. He can get too stuck in being unhappy, truly believing he is, where the unhappiness is not the result of any real sadness but is a sadness invented to get sympathy.

Caleb may begin a pattern of being a victim, always feeling victimized.

Since being a victim brought good stuff (hugs), he may regularly seem to find himself a victim, unconsciously preferring the role of victim over working out solutions. It is a bad pattern to encourage.

Rather than looking for a solution, I would prefer to be miserable and get stuff.

Do not think for a minute that the above way of thinking is not a little bit present in all of us and very much present in some of us.

Last, if Caleb's pain at being belittled by a sibling, which can hurt his feelings but is definitely not terrible, gets lots of special attention and consideration, he can develop an exaggerated sense of the importance of his feelings compared to those of others.

Others may suffer, but nobody understands how much greater my suffering is.

The parents' role is to respect and give solace where their children have bad feelings. But this needs to reflect reality.

I will give more sympathy, more concern, regardless of my child's apparent response, on missing out on a long-anticipated trip to an amusement park than his not going to the Dairy Freeze that we just went to two nights ago.

I will give more sympathy for my child having been meanly teased at school by a group of classmates than for his having been teased by a sister.

Parents need to respond appropriately to the hurts of their children. This means responding according to what in your adult judgment is the true degree of hurt, not to how vehemently your children may be expressing their upset.

How should Caleb's mother respond?

There is no single perfect response, but she wants to be sympathetic—to a point. She does not want to get in the middle between Caleb and his sister; does not want to bring herself into it at all. She in effect wants to say, "Gosh, that must have been unpleasant, the problem *you* were having with your sister."

Then Caleb would learn—which is what you want—that when Ivanna puts him down he can go to his mother for comfort, but she won't get involved with what went on with him and his sister. He has to deal with Ivanna on his own. If he doesn't like what is happening between him and Ivanna, he can leave. That is always an option. Sometimes he will choose not to. Sometimes he might retaliate. He might find that doing so seems to take much of the sting out of his sister's barbs. He might do it again. Perhaps the resultant bickering would get out of hand, to the point that the children's parents would have to get involved in order to end their fighting. But what will evolve, if parents do not get in the way too much, is that Caleb will develop his own way of dealing with his sister's put-downs.

"I don't draw like a baby. You draw like a baby."

If left to their own devices, siblings develop a certain toughness, a counterpunching ability that enables them to handle on their own the verbal jabs of older siblings. They do not always have to be the victim. Obviously, this toughness, this not taking everything to heart, this not taking everything personally, is extremely useful in going out and dealing with the world. We want our children to be able to stand up for themselves; in the face of hostility they should not always crumble in despair. Caleb's mother would want this ability for her son. She would want him to get such training. And what better training than having to deal with a verbally abusive older sister like Ivanna?

"Caleb, everything you do is stupid."

"Everything you do is stupider."

If the abuse seems too much, parents can always end it by separating the two. But regardless, Caleb learns in his own way how to deal with a sister.

"You're a butt brain."

"*You're* a butt brain."

Self-Esteem

What goes on between siblings exists mainly in a realm separate from self-esteem. It is a realm that is far more about getting stuff, competition for attention, competition for space. We care intensely that our children grow up with a good sense of self-worth, self-esteem. If a sibling calling you a retard does not really affect your self-esteem, where does self-esteem come from? What is it?

Self-esteem is something we carry around with us.

I'm a winner. I'm a good person. People like me.

Whatever it is, self-esteem is pretty simple to describe. It is this thing inside of us that allows us to feel good about ourselves and gives us confidence in going out and dealing with the world.

"Bobby, you're sure about going to Camp Selden? You know you're not going to know anybody."

"That's okay. It looks like they have cool stuff. I'm sure I'll make friends, I always do."

Self-esteem is particularly useful for when things go badly.

The group of kids I'm with at camp knew each other from before. They don't seem real interested in being my friends. It kinda sucks. But maybe it'll get better. Maybe I can find some friends in another group.

Rather than: *Camp sucks. Nobody likes me. It's always like this for me.*

How does a child get self-esteem? Three separate factors

contribute. One is what you are born with. Different kids, different innate temperaments. You know the huge differences between your children that cannot be explained by how they were raised. Some kids are by nature buoyant and outgoing; others are more cautious, more liable to withdraw. Some seem more able to be happy being on their own, while some always seem to require others to help them pass the time. Some are more placid, easygoing, while others are clearly more high-strung.

My Stephen was always shy. Even in his play groups he kind of stayed to himself. And anywhere new he would stay next to me like glue. But his sister Marilyn, Miss Sociable, always went right up to people. We were on a trip and stopped at a public pool and in ten minutes she had made buddies of all the kids there. Stephen hardly went in the pool; he just hung around with us, playing his stupid video game.

The second source of self-esteem starts at birth and comes from nurturing, from being loved, being made to feel special, being paid attention to through the course of childhood by at least one consistent parenting figure. Gradually this love received goes inside the child to form an internal core of good feeling—the little potbellied stove at the core of the personality I referred to earlier. This core becomes a capacity to make ourselves feel good, an internal sense of solidity that with time allows us to blunt and ultimately overcome the frustrations and bad feelings that life throws at us rather than being dragged down by them.

This is a parent's number one role as a contributor to his or her child's self-esteem: nurturer.

There is a third source of self-esteem.

Four-year-old Billy had two wonderful parents who loved him to pieces. But he had always been behind his peers in skill development. This was noticeably apparent when he went to day care and was with the Birney twins who were about his age, or when he was with his same-age cousins, or with a couple of kids in the neighborhood who were approximately his age. Nonetheless, despite his shortcomings, Billy was a bubbly, happy little boy.

Now eleven, Billy still has two wonderful parents who love him to pieces. But he continues to lag significantly behind his peers in skill development, and though his classmates are usually nice to him in school, he has no regular friends. Billy is no longer such a happy boy.

The last major source of self-esteem comes from something altogether separate from parent love. It comes from a sense of our own competence in dealing with the world—good or not at sports, school, drawing, doing card tricks—and to what extent we feel that our skills are valued by the world out there, especially our own peer group.

Gradually over the course of childhood, parent nurturing loses much—but very definitely not all—of its power as a source of self-esteem.

"Gretchen, we think that you are a very special girl," says Gretchen's mother to her fifteen-year-old daughter.

"Yeah, yeah, yeah." Gretchen still does like to hear her mother's praise, but it just doesn't cut it like it used to.

But though the active role of parent nurturing decreases, the core, already in place, remains—forever—as a central piece of their self-esteem. Nonetheless, as children get older, nurturing alone is not enough; they also need accomplishment and acceptance by the world out there.

What is a parent's role in this last source of self-esteem? Parents need to teach skills. How to tie your shoes. How to ride a bike. Children who are regularly exposed to reading at home do far better in reading skills in school than those who are not. But teaching is not the exclusive domain of parents. It is also very much the role of the world out there. Hence an important role for parents is to regularly expose their children to new challenges, to push them out into this greater world beyond home and family.

Last, and of great importance, is helping them develop frustration tolerance, the ability to persist rather than quit. But also the ability to take losses, to accept no and move on. This comes from encouraging children when they have difficulty. It also comes from saying no when that is appropriate and from making demands that maybe they do not always feel like meeting. It actually damages them if they are regularly too successful in bullying or being so pathetic that you back down. How can they develop frustration tolerance if they are constantly successful at undoing every instance in their day-to-day life when they are not getting their way?

"But I can't. I can't. Why do you always make me? It's not fair. I'm too tired. You're not fair. I hate you. You don't understand."

"Oh, all right."

"You're a good daddy."

———

Where does self-esteem come from? It comes from a child's own innate nature. It comes from feeling unconditionally loved and special in the eyes of a parent and from feeling competent in and accepted by the world.

My main point in all of the above is that what is not particularly a source of self-esteem is whether or not your sibling regularly told you that your breath smelled.

Not All Aggression Is Bad

This is a true story, and I think an important one.

It was a beautiful summer afternoon. I was out back working in the garden. Nick, who was ten or eleven at the time, was on the other side of the house playing basketball with his friend Gordon from down the street. It was just the two of them. Both Nick and Gordon liked basketball and were seriously into the game. Working in the garden, I could hear but not see them playing.

Over the course of about an hour, mainly what I heard was not the bouncing of a basketball, not the sound of a basketball hitting a rim or a backboard. Mainly what I heard was:

"No way! No way! Fuck you!"

"No, fuck you!"

"No, fuck you, you're an asshole."

Or words generally to that effect. My memory, and maybe this is distorted, but maybe not, is that over the course of the hour during which Nick and Gordon played basketball, there were maybe five minutes of the sound of a bouncing basketball and fifty-five minutes of shouting, arguing, and swearing.

I may have at some point gone around front, but if I did, my memory is that it was clear that Nick and Gordon had no interest in my getting involved. As far as they were concerned, everything was well under control. They were playing basketball.

Anybody who plays basketball, especially if they play any kind of informal pickup games that do not use referees, knows what this was about. Nick and Gordon *were* playing basketball. They were at that stage of basketball-playing development that works on the crucial step of establishing what are and are not fouls and other game violations like traveling (taking too many steps with the ball without dribbling). They were working on how to play basketball with other people who often are strangers, maybe to each other as well, and without a referee. They were learning how to do this and still be able to play a highly competitive game—really trying, really wanting to win—without it constantly breaking down into arguing or even flat-out fighting. Of course, even with those who have played a long time, serious fights can develop anyway. But overall, most experienced basketball players can get into a game with friends or strangers, play hard against these others who also are playing hard, play repeated games, all with limited—or no—arguing. The game continues.

But you cannot get to that point without first going through the stage that Nick and Gordon were at. Back and forth, playing and arguing, gradually defining the limits of exactly how much physical contact is acceptable, what really is a foul, what should be called traveling, what is not quite traveling.

Why do the vast majority of players work this out? Because they are joined by the same goal. They want to be able to play basketball, try really hard, have the other person try really hard, and thereby—and only if these conditions are met—have fun.

Maybe not all back-and-forth between siblings is bad. Maybe there is some good in being able to fully throw yourself into an interaction with another—keep it within certain bounds—and have the interaction move forward. Maybe it makes for more of a relationship. Maybe it makes for more of a life.

4. → Day to Day— What to Do

Some Classics

K. J. Took My Feather Pen

Theresa comes to her mother.

"K. J. took my feather pen and he won't give it back."

With this there are two options: You can get involved or not. I recommend not.

Not getting involved:

"Gosh, that's too bad."

"But he took my pen."

"Gee, I'm sorry."

"But you have to do something. Make him give it back."

"Golly, you're just going to have to work it out with K. J."

"But I can't. He won't give me back my pen."

"I don't know what to say to you, Theresa."

"Make him give me my pen back."

What usually happens now is that Theresa's anger switches fully toward her mother, because she is refusing to get involved.

"You never do anything. It's not fair. You don't know. You *have to* make him give me my pen. Mom! Mom! You have to."

And at this point, Theresa's mother wants to disengage.

"I don't know what to say to you."

"But you have to. You have to do something. It's not fair."

Theresa's mother must be firm. She has nothing more to say.

"But you have to. You do. You have to."

Actually, if it has been a regular policy that the children's mother does not get involved in such situations, Theresa may test her mother to see if maybe this time she'll yell at K. J. But if it is immediately clear that her mother, as always, is staying out of it, Theresa won't test very long. Early in the above sequence she would stomp off.

"You never do anything about K. J. and he ruins my life. He does."

But this is an exit line as Theresa goes off to deal with—or not—her obnoxious brother.

If Theresa is left to her own devices, there are many possible outcomes.

Theresa pursues it. "Give me back my pen."

Or Theresa goes to her brother's room and picks up

a leather wristband. "You're not getting this back until you give me my feather pen."

Or, "Fine, I'll never let you use anything of mine again."

With all of the above, either the two siblings would end up in a big fight where their mother would have to intervene— separating them, but very definitely not listening to what was going on.

Or, as becomes especially more likely if both brother and sister know that their mother will not get involved, they do work it out.

"Fine, here's your stupid pen." K. J. throws it across the room.

"If you broke it, you'll have to pay for it."

But they move on.

The other alternative is that the children's mother does get involved.

"Mom! K. J. took my feather pen and he won't give it back."

"K. J.! Get in here. I want you to give Theresa back her feather pen! Now!"

This way sounds clean and simple. In truth, however, it is the well-known call to dinner for the hungry baby alligators. With this option—no way around it—the children's mother immediately opens up and thereby places herself inside a whole other universe. With real-life children who are not afraid of their parents, what the children's mother will get is:

"Give Theresa back her pen, now."

"But she hit me."

"I did not. Besides, K. J. wouldn't stop bothering me."

"She never lets me use anything."

"Because you wreck it."

"Make her apologize for hitting me."

"K. J., give Theresa back her pen."

"It's not fair," says K. J. as he glowers and grips the pen more tightly.

"You heard me, K. J."

K. J. says nothing.

"Then you can forget about TV tonight."

"It's not fair. Theresa hit me. Mom, it's not fair."

And on and on.

And in the children's heads, as always, when their mother intervenes on one side or the other:

Theresa: *If K. J. bugs me, I can always use it to get Mom on my side.*

K. J.: *That little brat, she just runs to Mom and I always get blamed.*

No, the children's mother does far better by not getting involved.

Wesley Said I'm Going to Get Brain Disease

Kendall comes to his father.

"Daddy, Wesley said I'm going to get brain disease because one of the fried clams I ate wasn't fully cooked."

Kendall's father should be sympathetic. He should assume that whatever went on (which he does *not* want to get the details of), Kendall is upset. Hence, sympathetically, "No, you're not going to get brain disease."

"But Wesley said a clam I ate wasn't fully cooked."

"You're not going to get brain disease. Wesley just likes to say things that will get you upset."

That's all Kendall's father should or needs to do. That's it.

Kendall's father definitely is not interested in finding out what exactly went on and what was said. Why would he want to know? Kendall is worried about brain disease. His father has done what he can to dispel those worries. Also, in the process, Kendall's father has given the useful-for-future-purposes message: *Maybe not everything Wesley says is true.*

Absolutely what the boy's father does not want to do is to go after Wesley.

"Wesley?"

"What?"

"Did you tell Kendall he was going to get brain disease?"

"No, he's lying and he's a little jerk."

"Please do not tell your brother that he's going to get brain disease. It upsets him. You may think it's funny, but he's young and he gets upset."

There is nothing useful about saying all this to Wesley.

Wesley already knows that his father doesn't want him to tell his brother he's going to get brain disease.

The whole point of it *was* to upset his brother.

Regardless of what his father might say, Wesley does think it is funny.

But the main reason it is a mistake is that, as always, what Wesley will think is: *Kendall did it again, like he always does. He goes crying to Dad and gets me in trouble.*

The only product will be more resentment.

When Kendall's father told his son not to worry, that his brother was just trying to upset him, he accomplished all that was useful—including giving Kendall help with future dire warnings from his brother.

"Oh, you didn't put a Band-Aid on that cut. It's probably too late now. It'll probably get infected and you'll get gangrene and they'll have to amputate that finger. Maybe your hand. Even your whole arm."

"Oh, shut up, Wesley. You're a big loser. You just say stuff to upset me."

"Don't say I didn't warn you."

"Shut up, Wesley."

Kendall goes off not seriously worrying. But he does get a Band-Aid for the cut.

Luther Keeps Making Faces at Me

Nadia: "Daddy, Luther keeps making faces at me."

This one is easy. Their father absolutely does *not* want to get into it. Again, this is a place for one of those friendlier versions of "I don't want to hear about it."

"Gosh, that must make you mad."

Or, "Would you like a hug?"

These replies, as mentioned, may get good results.

"Yeah, I'd like to smack him in his face—hard. I hate him. I really do." But having vented her frustration, Nadia seems satisfied and moves on.

Or Nadia goes over and gets her hug.

But Nadia is after bigger fish. So she brushes off the compassionate response.

"But Dad, he's making faces at me."

That is: *Don't you understand? I don't want love and understanding. I want you to give me something or make Luther suffer, or preferably both—all of which will show that you like me better than him.*

But no way does Nadia's father want to intervene.

"Gosh, it's a problem."

"You never listen to me. All you care about is him."

Again, if Nadia's father's consistent message is that he is not going to get involved, Nadia will back off. And she will back off sooner than with anything else he might do.

"You don't understand. You never understand. Luther is the biggest brat in the world." Nadia shuffles off.

And not only will she drop the complaints more swiftly, but—getting nothing in response—Nadia is far less likely to bring them to her father in the first place.

Dad is no help at all. I'll have to deal with him myself.

"NNNN."

"Dad, Nadia is making the *NNNN* noise at me."

Lila Won't Give Me a Turn on the WhirlyCycle

Lila and Darren's parents had recently bought a Whirly-Cycle. They had made it clear when they brought it home from Mammoth Mart that the WhirlyCycle belonged to both kids. They would have to learn to share it.

It was a bright summer day, perfect for riding the Whirly-Cycle on the sidewalk and up and down their driveway. Darren came over to his father, who was trying to fix the front screen door.

"Lila won't give me a turn on the WhirlyCycle. She's hogging it."

As always: Don't get involved.

"Gosh, I'm sorry."

"But you said we'd have to share it, and she's not sharing."

"I guess you'll have to work it out with her."

"But I can't. She won't give me a turn."

This is an important example. In general the rule is that you don't want to get involved. You want the responsibility for working out the sharing to fall back on them. But sharing was a stated condition of getting the WhirlyCycle. And let's say Lila *was* hogging, not giving her younger and smaller brother a turn. Further, their father was right there and could not help but notice that Lila was the only one riding the WhirlyCycle. Because he made the rule that they were sup-posed to share—and clearly they were not, and because he was right there witnessing it—he can intervene.

"Lila, you have to give Darren a turn now. And not a real short one, either."

"But my turn isn't finished."

"Lila, give Darren a turn, now."

That is, if it is a stated sharing rule and you are right there observing the rule not being complied with, you can enforce it.

But still, how much monitoring of the sharing should their father do?

Let's say that after a while he went inside. A little later Darren came running to him again.

"Lila's not sharing. Make her give me a turn."

Their father has a choice. If he wants to make sure that his children always share the WhirlyCycle, he will have to regularly supervise the sharing. But over time that role can demand considerable time and energy. Maybe a more realistic and better aim in regard to siblings sharing is not that they share perfectly all the time, but that they understand that they *should* share. And where day-to-day sharing is required, it is their job to work out solutions on their own that do not always need parental involvement.

How will they learn about sharing?

In those situations where you are directly involved, they will share.

"I want you to equally divide up the french fries. No, that's not equally."

"Dad! It was too sharing."

"No, you gave your brother two french fries."

"But they were big."

More important, as discussed in regard to fairness, sharing will become a part of your children's character if they know you believe that it's right. And by your being a loving and unselfish parent, they get to internalize your caring for others—them—as part of themselves. As they accept you, so they are more likely to accept your beliefs as their own.

But for most day-to-day sibling sharing situations, you want to turn it back to them.

Darren's father decides not to intervene: "I guess you'll have to work it out."

"But I can't. She won't give me a turn."

"I'm sorry, Darren, you'll just have to work it out with Lila."

Darren then can either resign himself to not getting turns, or, as more often happens, he goes back to his sister.

"Dad said you have to give me a turn. He said we have to share."

"I will when my turn is finished."

"But your turn is forever. I want a turn now."

"Get out of here. My turn isn't done."

Perhaps noisy fighting ensues, escalating to a point where their father intervenes.

"Okay, the two of you. If you can't share the Whirly-Cycle without fighting, that's it for the WhirlyCycle for today."

Lesson to Darren: *If I make a fuss, Lila loses the Whirly-Cycle, which I'm not getting turns at anyway.*

Lesson to Lila: *If I don't at least share some—enough to*

satisfy the little baby—he'll fuss so much that I'll lose any chance at the WhirlyCycle at all.

Who knows how they will ultimately work it out? But as always, in the long run it is much better for them to be able to work through conflicts on their own, rather than your forever trying to impose solutions.

But It's My Turn to Sit on the Driver's Side

Macy's brother Kelvin had jumped into the backseat of the car and was sitting by the window on the driver's side. Macy was standing outside having a fit.

"Mom, he can't do that. It's my turn to sit on the driver's side. Kelvin, move over! Mommy, make Kelvin move over."

The children's mother didn't actually have a clue whose turn it was.

"Kelvin, is it Macy's turn? If it is, I want you to move over."

"No, it isn't," smiled Kelvin.

Macy looked like she was going to explode. "He's lying. He's lying. You're a liar. Mom, he's lying."

Kelvin just smiled and sat.

"Mom! Mom!"

If you're going to have a turns rule, you'd better be willing to keep track. But let's say, like most people, the children's mother did keep track, sort of. So what should she do in this instance where she really isn't sure whose turn it is?

The earlier-stated rule: If there is unpleasant fussing

going on—even if only one child is doing the fussing—intervene fast. Speed, not absolute fairness, is the priority.

"Macy, it will be your turn on the way back."

"No, it's not fair. It's not fair. Daddy will know. Call him on his cell phone. He knows it's my turn."

No, Macy's mother did not want to call their father on his cell phone.

"But it's not fair. It's not."

"Macy, get in the car."

"I can't. I won't. I hate you. You're unfair."

And the whole ride Macy stayed in a major snit.

"It's not fair. It was my turn."

Macy learned two lessons: *Sometimes Mommy is unfair and there is nothing I can do about it. All I get for the unfairness is nothing. No justice.* That is: *Sometimes life is unfair.*

And: *I guess Mommy doesn't really care that much about who sits where. All she cares about is that she hates fussing.*

Later, "Daddy, Mommy let Kelvin sit in the best seat and it wasn't his turn."

"Would you like a hug?"

"No, I want you to yell at Mommy and take something away from Kelvin."

In the Car (and Out in Public)

Three children are riding in the backseat of a car being driven by their father.

"Rusty's not staying on his side."

"Ow! Dad, Pat pinched me."

"Get off my side!"

"You little bitch."

"Ow! Dad, Rusty pinched me."

"Noah!"

"Ow!"

Cars present a special problem. The problem is that you're trapped. Not listening is fine, but in a car it's hard not to listen when they are right on top of you and you can't escape. The rule, already stated, is that when sibling bickering starts to irritate you, it's time to intervene, which requires separating the combatants. But separation is not an option in the car.

"That's it. Rusty, out of the car. This is where you get off."

"But I don't know where we are or how to get home and I'm only seven years old."

"Well, you should have thought of that before you started pestering your sister."

Not an option.

So what do you do, especially since sometimes sibling fighting in the car can become a serious distraction to you, the driver? It can actually turn into a safety hazard.

In general, try to ignore what goes on as best you can. But if it really becomes too much, there is an option, which many parents use. When it is first safely possible, pull to the side of the road.

"Okay, we're not going anywhere until you all calm down."

Then say no more and wait.

What almost always happens is that, when they see that you mean business, in a relatively short period of time they settle down. You then start back on the road.

The technique works. But it does not stop them from eventually starting back up again.

This strategy has a number of uses. The strategy is: *Nothing moves forward until the fussing stops.* It applies where you are involved with your children in some sort of ongoing process and their behavior has become increasingly unpleasant. You simply stop whatever you are doing, disengage from them, and wait.

"We are not going anywhere, not doing anything, until the fussing stops."

One place that this technique becomes particularly useful is when you are out in public.

Jason, Joshua, and Jana were constantly bickering while on a clothes shopping trip to the mall. The bickering was now getting out of hand. Again, separation was not an option.

"Okay, Jason, you will have to stay in Just for Kids while the twins and I finish our shopping."

"But I'm only seven and I'll be scared of kidnappers."

"Well, you should have thought of that before, shouldn't you?"

Again not an option.

Wherever you are, stop—sit if possible, or, if not, stand—and wait.

"We're doing nothing more until all of you calm down."

Then you stay where you are, say no more, and wait.

Same as with the car, this works. Usually not immediately, but they will calm down. And then you continue.

On a long outing, you'll probably have to repeat this technique more than once. But it works, and it works better than anything else you might do—lectures, threats, punishments, what have you.

It is a particularly valuable technique for what can be grueling family outings—trips to zoos, museums, and amusement parks.

"We almost got through the day until Daddy totally lost it and handed Reggie to the *T. rex* on the Journey Through the Jurassic dinosaur ride."

I am not a fan of going home as a solution. For one, it gives too much power to the kids. If they don't like what's going on, they can fuss enough to make you leave.

I also don't like it because it's inconvenient.

I really don't have the time to come back on a different day. I know it would be easier to shop with one at a time, but it's too hard figuring out what to do with the others.

But maybe above all, you want to be able to go into public places with your children, not have it be something you dread. This will never be accomplished by leaving them home. Behaving in public takes practice. What are the limits of what they can do? Where is the line about what you consider acceptable behavior in public? You want to be able to go places with your children. The only way to have this happen is to keep doing it.

It's Not Fair

It's Not Fair! Adam Got the Blue Watermelon

When he was leaving the hardware store, Adam and Samantha's father noticed free taffy roll-ups in a plastic container. He grabbed two and then drove home.

"Hey, kids. Here, each of you can have a roll-up that I got for free from the hardware store," said their father, handing one to each child.

"It's not fair! Adam got the blue watermelon and all I got was the yucky grape."

"Well, it's mine now and I'm not giving it to you," said Adam.

"But Dad, it's not fair."

"I'm sorry, Samantha, I just picked up what they had."

"But why did Adam get the blue watermelon? He always gets the good stuff and I never do. It's not fair."

The rules of fairness dictate that their father should do one of the following:

1. Cut each roll-up in half and give each child half of each flavor.

2. Take back the roll-ups and distribute them by a chance method, such as putting one in each fist and letting the kids choose a fist.

3. Go back to the store—a five-minute drive—and try to get another blue watermelon one.

4. Establish some sort of IOU for Samantha so that the next time in a similar circumstance she gets her preference.

All of the above choices satisfy the standards of fairness. (I'm not crazy about the going back to the store option.) But there is yet another option that has nothing to do with fairness. It is what happened in this particular instance.

Arbitrary Parent

"Who's that?"

Suddenly, apparently out of nowhere, there appeared in the room a man dressed in an odd red-and-blue costume with a short cape and with a big *A* emblazoned on his front.

"Who're you?" asked the children's father.

"I'm Arbitrary Parent."

"Huh?"

"I'm Arbitrary Parent. I come to the rescue when it looks like parents are about to be mugged by fairness. I'm taking over now, kids. Samantha, you get what you got, and Adam gets what he got, and I'm sorry, Samantha, if you don't like what you got, but that's it."

Arbitrary Parent then vanished just as suddenly as he came.

"I don't like Arbitrary Parent," said Samantha. "He's not fair."

"I like him," said Adam, chewing on his blue watermelon taffy.

It is good to try to be fair. But you don't always have to be.

Fairness is good. But for that reason fairness is also the number one weapon that children bludgeon their parents over the head with when they are not getting their way. It is an effective weapon because parents want to be fair. But as discussed repeatedly, very often efficiency rather than strict fairness needs to be a parent's top priority.

It's Not Fair! You Always Let Caitlin . . . Do Rules Always Have to Be the Same?

"Tracy, please take the cups and plates and put them into the dishwasher."

"But I'm tired. I'll do it in the morning. I promise."

"No, Tracy, I want you to do it now."

"But it's not fair. Last week you said it was okay when you told Caitlin to bring the clothes down to the washer and she said she would do it in the morning and you let her."

Do the basic rules of parenting state that you must always be consistent? Are you answerable to your children always to be fair? If the answer is yes, you are in big trouble.

Let's say that Tracy is right. Five days before, in a similar situation, her mother had allowed Caitlin to put off a chore until the next morning. Sometimes there are good reasons for such seeming unfairness. Let's say Tracy's mother planned to run the dishwasher right then, so that she needed the cups and plates put in the dishwasher now, whereas with Caitlin five days ago she was not going to do the wash until the next day.

"No, Tracy, I need it done now because I'm just about to run the dishwasher. With Caitlin and the clothes it could wait."

Tracy might still balk at doing the chore, but now the fairness issue is no longer valid because her mother explained why the situations were not comparable.

But what if it really were unfair? Let's say that there was no urgency about bringing in the plates and cups, the dishwasher was not going to be run until the next day. The bottom line is that, no, you do not always have to be consistent or fair. You want to be consistent. You want to be fair. Overall it is something that you aim for. As discussed, for important matters fairness does need to be a strong consideration. *Marianne and Norah each got to have a nice birthday party with friends invited over. But Sam's had to be canceled at the last minute because their mother had to go into the hospital for emergency surgery. A month later, their mother now fully recovered, Sam got to have a delayed birthday party.*

For most day-to-day fairness situations, you want to be fair, but you don't want to let fairness be the absolute dictator of your actions. Your kids, however, would not agree.

"No, she has to be fair. It's the law."

"But you seem to care about fairness only when it's to your advantage," we observe.

"What's your point? Besides, who asked you? It's none of your business. This is between me and my mother."

As discussed, if overall you genuinely seek to be fair, that is plenty good enough.

The disaster comes if you let "It's not fair" have too

much power. If Tracy's mother wanted, she could say, "Okay. Just make sure that you do it in the morning."

That's fine. But the decision to allow Tracy to postpone the task should be based on the mother's not minding that Tracy put it off until morning, *not* based on the fairness issue. Suppose Tracy's mother just did not feel like having the task postponed. Tracy always asked to postpone tasks. Her mother wanted it done now. In that case, she should insist, even though Tracy was right that in a comparable situation with Caitlin, her mother had done otherwise. Tracy's mother's decision should not be based on what she did or did not do with Tracy's sister.

"What's this, Tracy?"

"This is a videotape of what you said to Caitlin last October thirteenth when she didn't want to put the dishes away."

They do have such videotapes in their brains. They can quote word for word, sometimes with real accuracy, sometimes creating pure fiction. But unless you have your own set of videotapes to counter the evidence of their videotapes— really, even if you do have the videotapes—you do not want to get into it.

What happens with real children in the real world, and this *always* happens, is that if they learn that "It's not fair" is an effective parent stopper, if they learn that in response to something that they do not like—for example, "Please put the plates and cups into the dishwasher"—the phrase can effectively cancel out the unpleasant request, you will never hear the end of it. Even if it fails to cancel out the unpleasant parent request, it may create a big screaming fight instead, getting the parent totally off the subject of the task at hand. If so, that will do just as well.

"Irwin, I have had it with you. I have *really* had it."

"I've really had it with you."

"Watch your mouth, young man."

If "It's not fair" gets too much leverage with parents, it becomes the permanent takeoff point for repeated endless fussing. For children it takes on a life of its own. The more effective it is, the more they come to believe it.

"They're not fair, they're not," sobs Ignacio. "Neville gets everything and I get nothing. I have to do everything and Neville just sits on his butt. They love him and they hate me."

Hooked up to a lie detector: "Do you really feel this way?"

"Yes, yes," sobs Ignacio, barely able to get the words out through his tears. The lie detector shows that he's telling the truth. Yet it is not real. Ignacio feels it is real at the time. Yet it is a product only of his frustration at not getting his way, which magically evaporates once whatever the issue was is no longer on the table.

Conversely, if parents overall try to be fair but do not respond to "It's not fair" when it regularly comes up in response to unpopular stances, something magical happens. The "It's not fairs" dramatically recede (though they never totally disappear). Failing to get leverage with parents, "It's not fair" loses favor and you get to hear it far less. This doesn't mean, however, that a child might not switch to something else to see if that works.

"I don't feel good. I really don't. I'm a little dizzy. Actually, I think I need to just sit here and watch TV and then maybe I'll feel a little better."

Not only will you hear it less, but your children's perceptions change as well. The cosmic unfairness that resonates to the core of their being recedes. They may at times still think about it, feel it, but by parents not regularly responding to it children actually feel less, not more, the victims of a parental system designed to give them the short end vis-à-vis their siblings. It really does work that way.

It's Not Fair! You Let Frankie Walk to RediMart

"It's not fair! You let Frankie walk to RediMart!"

This was true, but Jamal's mother was not comfortable letting two-years-younger Jamal walk there by himself. There were a number of streets to cross, including Longview Avenue, which was a major thoroughfare.

Here the rule is: *What you do in regard to one sibling should not be inextricably tied to what you do with another.* It follows that the most obvious response—"When you're as old as Frankie, you can walk to RediMart"—may not be the best.

Some children are more mature, more responsible than others. It could happen that when Jamal reached the age at which Frankie was allowed to walk alone to RediMart, Jamal was still too impulsive, far less responsible than Frankie was at that age. At the same age, Jamal's mother was still not comfortable having him walk alone to RediMart. She does not want to tie herself to promises she might not want to keep. But remember, Jamal has a videotape of the promise.

"But you said that I could walk to RediMart when I was Frankie's age, and he was nine and now I'm nine. So you have to let me walk to RediMart."

"Yes, well, I know I said that, but I didn't absolutely promise it."

Hence I prefer: "Someday you will be able to walk by yourself to RediMart, too."

"When?"

"When I decide that you're ready."

"When's that going to be?"

"When I decide that you're ready."

Not only do rules for each child not have to be comparable at each age, but children are different, situations are different. You do not want to be tied down in what you do with one child by what you have done with another.

Rhonda and Ronald were twins. Their mother trusted Rhonda to be alone in the house, but not Ronald.

"It's not fair. You let Rhonda do it."

"I'm sorry, I don't want you to be alone in the house."

"But it's not fair. Rhonda gets to and I'm thirteen minutes older than she is."

Ronald's mother could offer the explanation: "I'm sorry,

I just don't feel as comfortable as I do with Rhonda that you won't get into trouble."

But it is best not to get into the comparison at all.

What goes on with you has to do with you. What goes on with Rhonda has to do with Rhonda.

"Someday you will stay alone in the house." (Unspoken: *But it will have nothing to do with whether I let Rhonda or not.*)

"But it's not fair. You treat me like a big baby."

You don't want to touch it.

"Someday you will stay alone in the house, but not now."

"But it's not fair."

If the fairness card really gets no response, Ronald will let go.

It's Not Fair! Ariana Got to Go Over to Her Friend's House

"It's not fair! Ariana got to go over to her friend's house, but you won't take me to Kirby's house!"

"I'm sorry, Tamara, that was yesterday. I am too tired today to drive you over to Kirby's house and pick you up."

"But it's not fair. Yesterday you took Ariana."

"I'm sorry, Tamara. I'm too tired. Maybe we can do it another day."

"But it's not fair."

This is a simple one. Tamara's mother *is* sorry that she's

too tired to take her over to her friend's house, but that she drove Tamara's sister the day before is not related to, is not part of the same universe as, her decision not to take Tamara today.

"But it's not fair."

"I'm sorry, Tamara."

There really is nothing more to say.

A further recommendation:

You do not want to be tied to always having to balance things out in the future. The fact that one day you drove Ariana to a friend's house, but the next day you didn't do the same with Tamara, does *not* earn Tamara IOU credits. Far, far better is that over time things even themselves out. You try to do well by all your children. You do *not* want to be tied to the great master list on the refrigerator.

"Mom, it's Mr. Pennyfield, the village wise man."

"Yes, I can see on the list: 'Two weeks ago Ariana got to stay up half an hour later for no special reason and nine days ago you yelled at Tamara but not Ariana for leaving her shoes in the hallway.' What would be fair, I think, to even the balance, would be for Tamara to be allowed to eat in the TV room for the next two days and not have to clean up, or for you to give her a dollar fifty. Yes, either would be fair."

"Well, I guess so. If you say so, Mr. Pennyfield."

"I want my dollar fifty."

It's Not Fair! Toby Got a Gerbil and I Didn't

For a long time, nine-year-old Toby had been pestering his parents about getting a gerbil. Finally they gave in, deciding that he was old enough and responsible enough to take care of the gerbil on his own. His seven-year-old brother Randy wanted to go along to Mel and Larry's Pet and Mattress City when they bought the gerbil. Randy seemed to have a good time, but as soon as they got home he started in.

"It's not fair! Toby got a gerbil and I didn't get anything!"

There is perhaps nothing that touches that special ravening place deep inside our kids—and, really, us as well—like other people getting stuff. Just the other sibling, the other person, getting something—anything—inspires a longing that we never knew was there.

"Arthur, look what I got."

"What is it?"

"It's a glow-in-the-dark bathtub rubber ducky. If you turn out the lights, it will glow in the bathtub."

"That's the stupidest thing I ever saw."

"You're just jealous."

"No, it's the stupidest thing I ever saw."

Then, without missing a beat, "Mom, why didn't you get me a glow-in-the-dark rubber ducky, too?"

"I thought you'd think it was stupid."

"I don't care, I want one."

And of course, if Arthur's mother did get him the glow-in-the-dark rubber ducky, he might use it once then relegate it to the recesses of his closet.

"I thought you wanted it."

"It's stupid. It's a baby toy."

"Then why did you insist that I buy it for you?"

"I don't know."

In regard to getting stuff, no matter what you do, if one gets something, the other is going to want something, too. This is normal. It is good to try to be more or less balanced. More or less the same on birthdays and holidays: If you go on a trip and get something for one, you want to get something for the other. Spur-of-the-moment treats should include everybody.

"Okay, each of you can buy a toy, but it can't cost over five dollars."

In regard to getting stuff, try to be more or less equal. That said, *more or less* means more or less. It does not mean exactly or every time.

Having finally decided that they would get Toby a gerbil, his parents could have waited until a time when there was something comparable that they were going to get for Randy. They could have decided that this was only fair. But they don't have to. This time it was about the parents' decision to get Toby a gerbil. That does *not* automatically mean that they have to get something for Randy. Having decided to get Toby a gerbil, they are not answerable to Randy that he did not get something. It was about Toby getting a gerbil. It was not about what Randy will or will not get.

Randy's parents might say, "Sometimes you get stuff—

remember your new hockey stick last week? But this time Toby is getting stuff."

But Randy already knows this. What he wants is to get something now, which is not going to happen.

"But it's not fair. Toby got a gerbil and I didn't get anything."

At this point Randy's parents really don't want to talk with him about *his* getting or not. This was about Toby getting a gerbil. To the extent that the boys' parents feel they must answer Randy because of what Toby got, they are saying—no way around it—that Toby's getting has to be tied in with Randy's getting. You do not want to encourage this connection.

If children see that their parents do not act as if they are absolutely answerable to a who-gets-what balance scale, the jealousy will always be there, but in day-to-day instances it will far more swiftly die.

It's not fair. Every time Toby gets anything, I should get something. But Mom and Dad are mean and they love him more than me, and no matter what I say they still won't get me anything. They are so unfair.

If the perceived unfairness gets them nothing, it fades away.

They do love him the best. They do.

But without much parental participation it gets hard to keep the sense of injustice going.

It is. They do.

What should Randy's parents say? As usual, make friendly comments, but ones that offer no possibility that you'll get involved.

"Gosh, you wish you got something."

"Gee, I'm sorry you're not happy."

"Would you like a hug?"

"No. It's not fair. It's not. I never get anything. You love Toby more than me."

If Randy's parents truly do not pick up on the unfairness issue, it will fade, more quickly than with anything else they might do.

"It's not fair. It's not."

Parent Court

"Hey, let's take it to Parent Court."

And so Reed and Serena went through the huge, ornately carved wooden doors that led into the Supreme Parent Court. There, as always, sitting on the high marble dais, was the supreme justice of Parent Court—Mommy. Actually, it wasn't exactly Mommy, it was as always a huge and incredibly delectable chocolate cake that was also Mommy, in her incredibly delectable chocolate cake form.

"Reed pulled my sweater."

"Serena hid my pencil."

The children screamed excitedly as they rushed up to Mommy and began grabbing at pieces of the cake that was her and shoving them into their mouths.

"Reed, what is the rule?" asked Supreme Justice Mommy.

"That you always favor Serena and never me. That's the

real rule," screamed Reed as he continued stuffing pieces of chocolate cake Mommy into his mouth.

"You liar, Reed. You get everything," screamed Serena as she, too, avidly stuffed the cake who was Mommy into her mouth.

After about twenty minutes, Supreme High Justice Mommy having been fully consumed, the brother and sister—full and happy—left the courtroom.

"Let's go back in ten minutes," said Serena.

"Cool," said Reed.

I feel like I've been eaten alive again, thought now-invisible Mommy, exiting Parent Court and resuming her normal shape.

Baby Self Favorites—When Are You Hearing Them?

You Love Vinnie More Than Me

"You love Vinnie more than me. You do. You do. You always loved him more than me. Everything is for him. It is. I know it."

We hook Derek up to a lie detector.

"Do you really feel that your parents love Vinnie more than you?"

"Yes. Yes. Yes, I do. They do."

The lie detector shows that Derek is telling the truth.

Nor is this the first time that Derek's parents are hearing this lament. Does Derek really feel that his parents don't love him, that they strongly prefer his brother over him? If so, they should be very concerned.

But there is a funny thing. These particular complaints seem to come up only at certain times. Namely, when Derek is mad at his parents because he is not getting his way.

Derek had wanted to replay a hole at miniature golf where he had done poorly. But his parents said no, they had to go on to the next hole. This meant Derek would probably lose to Vinnie, and he had a fit.

Derek had wanted to watch *Revenge of the Vampires* on TV and his parents wouldn't let him.

Derek had dawdled and the family was late getting out of the house and his parents yelled at him.

These would be the times when they would hear Derek's lament.

"You love Vinnie better than me," he would sob.

But at other times they did not hear any of this. In fact, were we to ask Derek at some other time, when he was in a good mood, no special ax to grind, "Do you think your parents love Vinnie more than you?"—in such circumstances, most of the time, he would say, "No, I know they love me. Sometimes I think they do favor Vinnie. I can name twenty-seven specific circumstances where this occurred. But, no, I think they love me and Vinnie the same."

Perhaps Derek perceives that there still might be some

advantage to saying that he thinks his parents love Vinnie better. Now further removed from the situation and no longer fully in the sway of his baby self: "No, they don't love me. They love Vinnie better."

Now the lie detector makes beeping noises.

"It's broken," says Derek.

But it is not. You may hear from your children how unfairly they feel they are treated, how unloved they feel, but before you take their words too seriously, you need to ask yourself a serious question: *When am I hearing this?*

If the answer, as so often is the case, is *When they are not getting their way,* you need to think long and hard before you take what they say too seriously.

If you worry, ask yourself whether you have ever heard it come up spontaneously in a completely neutral time where your child had nothing to gain from his or her complaints. And if you still worry, ask. But make sure that it is at a time and in a situation where your child sees no strategic gain.

"Do you really feel we love Vinnie more than we love you?"

"I dunno. I guess not. But Vinnie always gets everything and I don't."

There is a fact about children when operating in their baby self mode. It is a fact that is neither good nor bad. It just is. In a way that makes no logical sense, but nonetheless is, children feel that what they say in their baby self mode *does not count.*

"How could you say that?"

"I dunno."

"How could you say that?"

"I was mad."

"How could you say that?"

"You yelled at me."

This means that there will be times where you will hear words out of your children's mouths that sound terrible but mean very little. Not only terrible to hear, but *intentionally* terrible. When not getting their way, the whole point is for their words to have maximum possible effect, and so they choose words that best push your particular buttons.

Let me mention some of the baby self's absolute favorites for such situations.

I Never/You Always

"I *never* get anything I want and Annie always does."

"I never" and its variant, "You always"—as in, "You *always* let Annie stay up and never me"—are high on the baby self's list.

Here, my main piece of advice is that you definitely want to resist the temptation to come back with, "But what about the time that you . . ."

If you say this, all is lost. She was waiting for that. She will always have an answer, and now that you have entered the fray, you immediately open yourself up to, "No, that didn't count because that was a delayed birthday present and also, what about when Annie got her red coat? What about that?"

Best as always is to be sympathetic.

"I know it makes you mad that sometimes Annie gets stuff and you don't."

But if this gets only, "No, I *never* get stuff," then it is time to say no more.

"But I don't. I never get anything. Annie always gets everything. She does."

You Don't Love Me

"No, I'm sorry, Will, but you have to go to bed now."

"But Nila got to stay up. It's not fair."

"Will, I want you in bed now."

"But it's not fair. It's not. You always favor her. You do. You don't love me. You don't." Tears now stream down Will's face.

There is a paradox about "You don't love me." For children, the actual serious thought that their parent would not love them is terrifying. Were a child ever to feel even the slightest doubt, he would never bring it up.

"You don't love me."

"Well, Henry, since you brought it up, you're right."

Far, far too scary.

It is precisely those children who feel absolute certainty in their parents' love, and only those children, who will say, "You don't love me."

I know you love me, which is why I say you don't love me because I know that since you do love me, it will get you very upset.

Hence, when it comes up at those times when a child is not getting his way, you do not want to touch it.

"You don't love me."

"I'm sorry, Will. It's time for bed."

I Hate You

"I hate you."

Actually, at that moment she does. She is not getting her way and it's your fault.

But you don't know. When she gets that look, I can see the hate.

Luckily, it doesn't last very long. Because the greater truth lies in the deeper, permanent part of her that does indeed love you. Very much.

Part of being an effective parent is being willing at times to go against the wants of your children. If you do, they at that moment will hate you.

Why can't they say something a little less mean, like, "I'm mad at you"?

It doesn't have the same pizzazz. An important reassurance to them is that they can get mad at you, even say very mad things, and lose nothing. You still love them as much as you always did.

But Why?

"Why? You have to give me a reason. Why?"

This is particularly annoying because it is relentless. Children can use it in response to anything—everything— you say.

Even if you are not planning to change your mind, it is always useful to give an explanation.

"No, I'm sorry. I know I let your brother see *The Revenge of the Dead Zombies*, but I feel you're too young. You think it won't upset you, but I know it will. And then you'll be too scared and wish you hadn't seen it. When you are older, you'll be able to watch all the scary movies you want. But not now."

"But why?"

Having given the best, clearest, most honest—but not too lengthy—response, the answer to the next "Why?" is no answer. Then move on even if he won't.

"But why? Why? I don't understand. Why?"

Property Rights

All children have a right to ownership of a certain part of the world that extends beyond their own bodies. This includes their possessions—their clothes, their baseball, their CDs, their toothbrush. Kids have a right to their own things and also their own space—a room or part of a room that they can decorate as they wish, where they can store their stuff, where they can hang out, and where, at times, they can be alone. Also, they should have a right to temporary control over a given piece of more public space where they, for the moment, can do what they want—their side of the couch, a part of the floor where they have set up their trucks, that space above the floor where their legs are hanging when they are sitting at the dinner table. Of course, it is over property and space that most sibling conflicts occur.

"Sharon keeps touching my leg with her leg."

"Cecily's wearing my sweater."

"David won't leave me alone."

Property rights should be stated.

"This is the space for Allison's toys. You have your own space."

"You may not wear Kimberly's clothes."

"Charles, stay on your side of the couch."

The problem comes with enforcement. To what extent do you want to spend your time and energy policing property violations?

You should enforce property rules if you directly see them being broken.

"Give Kimberly back her sweater. You'll have to wear something else."

"Andrew, get away from Allison's cupboard. You're not to go in there unless she says it's okay."

But more often than not, you are not there to immediately witness a clear violation of property rules. Most of it is hearsay.

"Mom, Cecily wore my sweater and now it's stretched."

"I did not and it isn't." ·

"Mom, David keeps coming on my side of the couch."

"Charles is lying. He's the one who keeps coming on my half."

The bottom line about property rules is that they should be clear. You should stand behind them. But unless you want to spend most of your time working on raising your blood pressure, children will have to work out most of the day-to-day property rule infringements on their own.

Brendan's Wrecking My Fort

Nine-year-old Elena was building an elaborate LEGO fort on the floor of the TV room.

"Brendan, get out of here." Elena's five-year-old brother Brendan had come over and was running two small toy trucks into Elena's fort.

"Brendan! Stop it. You'll wreck my fort."

Brendan ignored his sister. Elena gave her brother a hard push, whereupon Brendan punched his sister. Elena then punched Brendan as hard as she could on his arm, at which point Brendan started to shriek.

In the next room, the children's father, who had been trying to glue together a decorative plate that had been broken, heard the shrieking and came into the TV room.

"Daddy, Brendan is ruining my fort."

"Elena hit me and made me fall down."

"But Dad, he keeps running his trucks into my fort and wrecking it."

The rule is that unless there is threat of harm—which here the children's father did not feel was the case—do not intervene on one side or the other.

"The two of you, that's it. Brendan, find somewhere else to play."

"But that's not fair. I wasn't hurting anything and Elena punched me real hard."

In this instance, the separation does favor Elena. She gets to stay and continue her playing unhindered by her brother. Her father had swiftly decided that Elena was already established playing where she was, and it seemed simplest and fairest to remove Brendan. Remember, interventions do not have to be totally fair to all parties. They just have to be fast.

Of course, if Brendan genuinely wants sympathy for the punch he got, that is always available.

"Do you want to come and sit on my lap?"

Which he might, though more often you'll get, "But she punched me and it's not fair"—that is, you are supposed to do something to her. "I was just trying to play with her."

Regardless, Brendan has to leave.

Let me mention an alternative.

"Elena, Brendan just wants to be part of what you are doing. See if you can figure out some way of including him."

"But he's just going to wreck it."

"See if you can include him."

I'm not against this. Sometimes it can work. But it does have a built-in risk.

"No, it's my fort. I'm working on it. I don't want to include him."

Then what? Their father insists? Then maybe Elena will grudgingly comply. But what if Elena flat-out refuses to include her brother? Does their father then have to bring in further consequences?

"Either include Brendan or neither of you gets to play with the LEGOs."

This really does seem unfair to Elena. She was working on the project by herself. Surely she has a right to do it on her own if that is what she really wants. If Elena genuinely does not want to, she shouldn't be forced to include her brother. Better might be a strong request, with the weight of his influence but with no consequences for Elena if she does not comply.

"Elena, I would appreciate it if you would include Brendan. He only wants to participate."

But if she adamantly refuses, then, "I'm sorry, Brendan, unless you can play here without making a fuss, you're going to have to be in another room."

"But it's not fair. Elena gets everything her way."

Which in this instance is true. But in this example other options seem too unfair to Elena.

The message to Elena: *I do have some rights in keeping Brendan out of my space.*

The message to Brendan: *If Elena is working on some-*

thing and I cross over into her space, I'm not going to get anything good out of it.

Cato Used My Toothbrush

Melody comes to her father. "Dad, Cato used my toothbrush."

As always, best is not to get involved.

"Golly, that must have made you mad."

"But, I'm going to get all his germs. Tell him not to. He's gross. He contaminated my toothbrush. Tell him not to."

"Gosh, it's a problem."

"You have to make him stop."

Cato already knows that he is not supposed to use his sister's toothbrush. She cares a lot that he not use it. But Cato couldn't care less which toothbrush he uses and typically grabs whichever is most convenient. Unless Melody wants to keep her toothbrush in her room, Cato will at times use her toothbrush. If their father wants, respecting Melody's wish for exclusive use of her toothbrush, he might at a separate time say something to Cato.

"I wish you wouldn't use your sister's toothbrush. It's hers. I know you don't care, but she does."

In saying this, their father must understand that his speaking to Cato will have some effect on his using his sister's toothbrush, but only some. Further, Cato's father is also noting that beyond his statement, he is going to do nothing more to enforce the toothbrush rule. *I wish you wouldn't use Melody's toothbrush, but I'm not going to do anything to stop you.* The one exception would be if Melody or Cato were sick and their father really did not want Cato using his sister's toothbrush, in which case he might temporarily supervise toothbrush use.

Otherwise, their father does not want to get involved. Regardless of any intervention, Cato will occasionally use his sister's toothbrush. If Melody knows that her father won't get involved, she probably won't even come to him. She will deal with her brother on her own.

"Cato, if you use my toothbrush again, next time we have cauliflower I'm going to put some of mine on your plate." Cato has a morbid fear of cauliflower contamination and will not eat any of his food if cauliflower has ever touched it.

"I'm gonna tell Daddy."

"Go ahead. He won't even see me do it."

This tactic by Melody will result in Cato still occasionally using his sister's toothbrush—just as with any other intervention that might have been tried by their father.

Tyler Keeps Bothering Me

"Hi, I'm Tyler. I get bored easily. I'm kind of hyper. It's okay watching TV or playing video games or even being outside digging holes, but mainly I get bored easily. I'm not so good at entertaining myself. Mostly I like to bother people. I especially like to bother my sister Johanna."

"Dad, Tyler keeps bothering me."

Tyler, bored, once again resorted to his fallback activity—bothering his sister. Sometimes Johanna was willing to play with Tyler, but most of the time she wasn't.

"No, Tyler, I don't want to play with you."

Or, "Tyler, please leave me alone."

Or, "Can't you find something to do by yourself without bothering me?"

All of the above rarely worked. Tyler was *very* persistent.

"But I'm bored. You have to do something with me."

Typically, things would then deteriorate to the point where they were yelling at each other, sometimes hitting. All of which was fine with Tyler—at least he did not have to play by himself.

"Dad, Tyler keeps bothering me. He won't leave me alone."

What to do?

Some of the time their father should ignore it, forcing Johanna somehow to deal with her brother on her own. But the fact is that there are some children—the Tylers of the world—who constantly intrude on the space of another sibling. And unfortunately, if left to fend off such a sibling on their own—to stake out at least some personal space—often nothing works. Here I think parent intervention is appropriate—not to take sides, but to separate. It is the only thing that will work, though only temporarily. Tyler will be back. Talks, rewards, punishments; all are singularly useless. They may work occasionally, but over the long haul they will not work at all.

There is a powerful force inside all Tylers.

"Tyler."

"What?"

"I want you to walk through this room, go through the door on the other side of the room, and I want you to do it without going over and poking your sister, who as you can see is sitting on the couch. Do you see what is in my hand?"

"Yeah, it's a twenty-dollar bill."

"It will be yours if you can do what I just said."

"Cool."

Tyler started across the room, but then made a detour and went over and poked his sister.

"Sorry, Tyler, no twenty dollars."

"But it's not fair. Johanna made a sort of face at me. Let me do it again."

A normal part of many kids is that there just is this pull. It is actually a part of their positive attachment to a sibling, very much like a magnetic field. And it is very strong. With some, the only answer is to regularly separate. It will work, but only for a while.

"Dad, Tyler poked me again."

The Phone, TV, Computer

"Andy, I have homework. I need to get on-line to look up some stuff."

"No, Trina, I'm in the middle of a game."

"Get off, now. I have homework."

"No, you can do it later."

"Get off, now!"

A major source of ongoing conflict between siblings is access to phone, computer, video games, television. The general rule for sibling disagreement is to let them work it out themselves. However, if they can't, if there is too much bickering, a parent has to intervene—taking no sides—and all have to deal with the consequences.

So, for example, "Okay, nobody uses it tonight."

"But Dad, I have homework."

"No, I'm sorry, next time you'll have to figure out how to settle it without this screaming."

"But Dad, what am I supposed to do? I have homework and Andy wouldn't get off the computer!"

Trina has a point. Trina's father would not be wrong to order Andy off the computer. Homework has priority over game playing, though Andy should be able to get his game-playing time, too. Maybe Andy was right. He would have gotten off the computer in fifteen minutes and Trina could have waited. There was no special reason that she had to start right then.

The problem is that if they cannot work it out between themselves, which in regard to electronic access often is the case, a parent is stuck constantly having to intervene. The world of electronics is today such an integral part of the home and of a child's life, and that world possesses such a powerful hold on children, that they often cannot work out solutions by themselves. If siblings are able to resolve those conflicts without adult supervision, fine. But if they cannot, you'll probably need to remove solutions from the arena of day-to-day negotiation and instead create ongoing set rules.

Here, discussion with your kids is useful. They can let you know what they want, what matters to them, what times work for them. Maybe together you can come up with a plan, a schedule, a set of rules that more or less satisfies everybody. But maybe together you can't. In that case you have to set the rules, rules that you reserve the right if necessary to change at any point, and change again.

If there is a schedule, for it to work, you have to enforce it.

"Dad, Andy's not letting me use the computer."

"No, you'll have to wait until eight o'clock when it's your time."

Or, "It's after eight and it's my time and Andy's not letting me use the computer."

"Okay. Andy get off the computer."

In regard to the world of electronics, it often works best for the parent to be both rule setter and also police officer.

Common Aggravations

Who Did It?

One afternoon the children's mother discovered a large puddle of orange juice on the kitchen floor.

"Erika, Matthew, Sammy, get in here!"

"What?"

"Who is responsible for the big puddle of orange juice in the kitchen? You know that if you make a mess like that you have clean it up fast before it starts to get all sticky so nobody will step in it. I am really mad. Which of you did it?"

"He did it."

"She did it."

"He did it."

"We're not going anywhere until the guilty party confesses."

"Tell her, Sammy."

"Tell her what, that you did it?"

Forget about finding out who is the guilty party. The culprit will never confess. It is not necessary, anyway, and the process of trying to root out the transgressor has only negative effects. I do not think it is useful for parents to put themselves in the role of grand inquisitor. It does not matter that the guilty party be officially blamed. What I recommend is as follows.

"I don't know who did it, but I have told you all repeatedly that if you spill, you have to clean up immediately. Whoever did it knows he or she did it, and that's who I am mad at. If you didn't do it, I'm not mad at you. Now I would appreciate it if you all help clean it up."

Simultaneously: "But I didn't do it. It's not fair."

"I don't know who did it, but I want all of you to help clean it up."

What does this accomplish?

Their mother's words restate for all with strong emphasis that spills need to be cleaned up right away.

Besides stating to all the children that this is important to her, their mother also provides the reasons why it is important to clean up spills immediately.

The guilty party knows that though their mother does not know who did it, his or her behavior in not cleaning up the spill definitely got their mother mad.

It's clear that in this household, all will at any given time be expected to participate in necessary tasks, and that participation is not based on particular rules of fairness but rather simply on need at the time.

It makes the perpetrator feel guilty. He knows he did it. He knows he was not supposed to do it, and he knows their mother is upset about it. If he has the normal very strong child-to-parent love attachment, he cares that his parent is upset about it. He *will* feel guilty.

Given all of the above, is there more that you want to accomplish?

Not only is the rooting out of the appropriate guilty person an unpleasant process often involving threats and possible punishments, it has one other very definite negative consequence. Where there is too much emphasis on which child is to blame, that focus actually gets in the way of the guilty party feeling guilt over what he did. It interferes with rather than facilitates his feeling responsibility for his actions. How is that? The problem with too much emphasis on blame, even where there is not some kind of punishment connected to it, is that the child's response to being on the wrong end is invariably to get defensive. They all do.

"Why do you always blame me and never Sammy? It wasn't my fault. It was an accident. You never notice when I do good stuff."

Anything to deflect the blame. The problem is that in the furious attempt to produce a thousand and one reasons why it wasn't their fault, they come to believe them. Best to stay focused on the crime—why it was bad and what needs to be done about it. The guilt will take care of itself. Honesty is not taught by punishing or yelling at a liar. If they are blamed, children lie. That's what they do. As with acting well, honesty is mainly taught by your being honest with your own children and by how honestly or not they see you deal with others.

I'm Telling

"I'm telling. Daddy!"

"What is it, Janelle?"

"Scott splashed water at me from the sink and now there's water on the kitchen floor and he's not cleaning it up."

I had a kind of joke rule with Nick and Margaret (not that I recommend it). If one of them told on the other, the one who got told on received a nickel.

Unless it is a matter of harm, one sibling tattling on the other is not something you want to encourage. What I recommend is as follows. If one tells on the other—even if it is about breaking a rule—the one who is told on will not get in trouble. Even if you believe the accuser, information from a tattle-telling sibling is inadmissible evidence.

I'm quite serious.

"Mommy, Elizabeth took a dollar out of your wallet."

Elizabeth gets in no trouble. In fact, I do not even mention it to Elizabeth. (But I do make a mental note not to leave my wallet lying around.)

"Daddy, Lucas said a lot of swears at Garnett when they were outside playing."

Their father does not like Lucas swearing, especially outside where neighbors can hear. But he says nothing to Lucas. Inadmissible evidence.

The problems with listening to tattle telling are many. For one, it assures ongoing friction between the tattler and the tattled on.

That little bastard, Edgar. I can't trust him for anything. He'll tell on me. He'll wish he didn't, because don't think I'm not going to get back at him.

You want them to be allies, at least occasionally feeling that they are on the same side, a bond between them. Regular tattling scotches any chance of that.

But the worse and more serious issue with tattling is not with how it affects the relationships among siblings. Most siblings do at least a certain amount of telling on each other.

"Jacob ate four of the cupcakes and now there aren't enough for everybody."

"Glenna said she cleaned the rabbit cage but she didn't."

Most siblings exist in a relationship that contains trust and mistrust simultaneously.

"I always tell on Daniel when he doesn't brush his teeth because I like to see him get mad. But I didn't tell the time he and Clement dared each other to throw a stone at Mr. Garibaldi's window and he did and it broke, because he really would have gotten into trouble."

The most serious problem with listening to tattling is not that it harms their relationship with each other. If they regularly tell, and you regularly listen, it hurts them.

"Mommy, Gerritt had his feet up on the couch with his shoes on again and got the couch dirty."

"Thank you, sweetheart. Boy, will Gerritt get in trouble now. I don't know what I would do without you. You're Mommy's wonderful little helper. But what are we ever going to do with that brother of yours? I suppose we have to keep him, but certainly I'll give you lots more good stuff than him. After all, I love you so much and I don't love him at all. Why should I, what with all the trouble he causes. Come here. Let me give you a big hug and then we can go shopping together and get more twinsy outfits."

"Mommy."

"What is it, Tim?"

"I saw Trisha smoking with her friend Leslie outside of Twenty-Four Pick Up."

"Thank you, Edgar. Here's your five dollars. You're still my good detective. Trisha!"

The above are exaggerations, but listening too well to tattlers gives them this exact same message.

Listening too well hurts the tattler because it creates a system whose point is to win the favor of those in power at the expense of others. Those who learn this system may do well out in the world with bosses who like toadying yes-men and -women. But these same people invariably end up wondering why so many others don't seem to like them.

Probably most damaging is that it is a system where self-esteem comes from being on the side of, getting approval from, those in power, not from one's own accomplishments. That is, *I on my own am nothing. Those in power are everything.* Listening to tattling teaches the exact opposite of personal integrity. Simply, it encourages the development of little sniveling scumbags.

What to do?

Definitely not, "Thank you for telling me."

But you do not want to criticize them either. What you want them to get from their tattling is nothing.

Best, as always, is to throw it back to them, in a nice but firm way.

"Gosh, I guess you didn't like that."

"But there's water on the kitchen floor and Scott isn't cleaning it up."

"You could clean it up if you want. That would be nice."

"But Scott was the one who splashed water on the floor and he's not cleaning it up."

At this point there really is nothing more to say to Janelle. For tattling on her brother Janelle needs to get nothing. And if the children's father wants the water cleaned up, he can do it himself or he can ask one or both of his children. But the children's father does not want to touch blaming Scott—it comes from an inadmissible source.

Little Parents

"Fritz, don't slouch like that. You should sit up straighter."

"Shut up, Mariel."

"I'm only saying it for your own good."

"Thank you, Mariel," said their grandmother, "but I'll worry about Fritz's posture. That's my job."

"But he's slouching."

"Shut up, Mariel."

"But he'll get bad posture."

"Thank you, Mariel, but I can handle it."

"I'm only trying to help, Grandma."

Some children seem to assign themselves the role of associate parent.

Well, Grandma needs my help. Fritz is never going to grow up right. She never says anything, and Fritz's habits are so disgusting.

"Fritz, don't pick your nose." *See what I mean?*

"Shut up, Mariel."

Why are some children like this? It could be about curry-ing favor with a parent. It might be about playing a role whereby you identify with a deeply admired person—your parent. It could be about trying to reject your own babyish impulses by playing out that internal struggle on an impul-sive, usually younger sibling. But mainly, I think, it is about bossiness.

"It's not that I'm being bossy. Fritz is a disgusting slob and Grandma is not doing anything about it. Somebody has to."

But it *is* about bossiness. Wanting to be bossy is not bad, especially if you can get away with it.

"No, I don't want to play it your way. I want to play it by my rules. Now I get three turns and you get one."

The only problem is that most people don't like to be bossed. So most children learn to compromise.

"Okay, we'll both get the same amount of turns, but be-cause it's my house I get one special bonus turn."

"That's stupid, Isabel."

"Please."

"Oh, okay."

A perhaps surprising fact about little parents is that big parents' attempts to discourage them seem to be consistently unsuccessful.

"Mariel, I know you want to help. But I'm the parent and not you. I know that some of the time what Fritz does both-ers you. But Fritz is my job."

"But you don't do enough. Look at the way he always walks on the back of his shoes"—which is true.

Mariel won't give up.

What to do?

Don't back her up, but don't try too hard to discourage her, either. You don't want Mariel's unwanted parenting help to be a constant source of negative attention for her. Of course if you are finding it too unpleasant, as with any unpleasantness, you can have her go elsewhere.

"Mariel, I find your correcting Fritz very irritating, so if you want to be here with me, you'll have to stop." *You can do all the parenting of Fritz that you want, but not around me.*

Mainly you just want to stay out of it, throwing Mariel's self-designated parenthood back to the mercy of her brother. That is, unless Mariel's grandmother is at that moment finding it too unpleasant to be around, what she should say is nothing.

"Fritz, don't shuffle your feet. Fritz, don't walk on the backs of your shoes. Fritz, you're ruining your shoes. Grandma and PopPop aren't made of money, you know."

"Shut up, Mariel."

Mariel will continue her self-appointed parenting. But as her parenting yields poor results with her recalcitrant brother—and as it also seems to yield no support or interest from her grandmother—it will tend to happen less.

Piggy for Attention

"Daddy, look what I made."

Clark had patiently pasted various small objects, most of

them little sticks and stones, onto a sheet of paper. There was no discernible pattern. The result was a collage of little stuff.

"That's really good, Clark. Is it supposed to be anything?" asked his father.

"Can I get a watch like my friend Irina has?" asked Clark's sister Tamika, who was standing nearby.

"Tamika, I'm talking with Clark. He's showing me what he made."

"But can I get a watch like Irina has?"

"Tamika, we can talk about that another time. I'm looking at Clark's collage."

"Do you want to see *my* collage?"

"Later. Right now I'm looking at Clark's collage."

"So why can't I get a watch like Irina's?"

"Tamika, I'm talking with Clark."

"But you never look at my stuff."

"That's not true, Tamika, but I am looking at Clark's collage now."

"No, you never do. You never look at my stuff."

All the while Clark sat patiently waiting for the focus to return to him and his art project.

This was not an unusual scene. Whenever Tamika's father paid any attention to either of her siblings, Clark or Sabrina, Tamika would immediately butt in and not leave off. It was as if she could not stand to have either of her siblings get one moment of undivided attention from their father. Tamika had to get the attention moved to her, even if—as usually happened—it ended up being negative attention.

Some kids are like this. They cannot bear to see the least bit of parent attention go to anyone but them. There can be many reasons why they are so piggy about parent attention. But regardless of why, the parent response should be the same.

Tamika's father wants to make sure that there are regular times where Tamika *does* get his undivided special attention. But *not* when he is paying attention to one of her siblings.

He should tell Tamika, as he did, that there will be other times that she will get his attention. She already knows this, but at the moment, craving everything, it is a useful reminder.

Then he should respond no more.

If Tamika persists in butting in, as is often the case, her father should say, "Tamika, you can stay here if you want, but you'll have to be quiet, because this is Clark's time. If you can't, you will have to leave."

If Tamika still persists and does not leave, her father can use the technique that does work. He simply sits and waits.

"Clark, we'll continue when Tamika leaves."

And then silence.

"Dad, this one time, please just look at my collage."

If her father has truly disengaged, Tamika will back off. If it is clear that she will get nothing more, she will either shut up or leave. Threats and punishments at this point are unnecessary and, in fact, often provoke more fussing. Tamika would have succeeded in getting attention, albeit negative.

But either—positive or negative—is fine with the true attention seeker. Her father's silent waiting is the same technique that I spoke of earlier for in the car or in public. *Nothing moves forward until you behave.* It works, and where parents use it regularly, their children learn that once their parent goes into the waiting mode, there is nothing more they're going to get. They calm down pretty quickly—though never immediately.

Tamika's father does not want to turn the focus onto her. If Tamika's demanding gets attention, any kind of attention, not only will it encourage continued fussing, but it is also bad for Tamika—it pulls her down. For responding to the insatiable demanding feeds it. It is a craving. But it is not a useful craving. As I have said repeatedly, in order to flourish, children need love and attention. But there is a part in all of us—the baby self—that wants not just what it needs but wants everything. If children are too successful at getting everything on demand, they cannot move on. And where children are too successful in bullying their parents into getting constant attention, they can get stuck. Instead of moving forward, instead of investing in pursuits beyond the exclusive focus on attention seeking, attention remains their primary goal. It gets in the way of maturing.

If you have an out-of-control passion for double ripple chocolate caramel fudge ice cream, it is not a good idea to have twenty half-gallon containers in your freezer. If you know it's there, there is no way your passion will not get the better of you. On the other hand, if your freezer has a locked time-release mechanism that dispenses one, and only one, four-ounce cup of double ripple chocolate caramel fudge in each twenty-four-hour period, you ultimately will resign yourself to the daily four-ounce cup. But only if you know—for sure, absolutely—that it is not possible to get more. Only after, for example, you unsuccessfully took an ax to the freezer and abjectly pleaded with the time lock company to reprogram the freezer release to two gallons a day.

"It's not for me. I'm having a party. It's for orphans. Did I say they are from Namibia?"

With children who constantly demand attention at the expense of their siblings, make sure that they get attention. But the attention should not be totally on their demand—they will never get all that they want—and it should not be at the expense of others. You want to give them enough. But enough is not everything—they do not need that.

Make Sari Stop Singing

"Dad, make Sari stop singing."

"But Max, she's just singing."

"Make her stop. It's so annoying."

"But she's not doing it to bother you. She's singing because sometimes she just likes to."

"You have to make her stop. It's making me deaf."

Why do they get so irritated? It can be about anything, like breathing, chewing, or laughing.

"Yes, that's another thing. I cannot stand how Sari chews. It drives me crazy. It's disgusting. It ruins my meals. And her laugh? Omigod."

For Max it is about his private space being filled against his will with an alien presence. And Sari really is not doing it to irritate him; she is genuinely happy and feels like singing— a nice thing.

But for Max, anything that simply declares that his sister is there is annoying. For him the words to the song are always the same.

I exist, I exist, and I'll shout my existence into all the spaces of your life.

I exist, I exist, don't you wish I didn't.

Why is it that roommates so swiftly start getting on each other's nerves? Why is it that good friends who go on long car trips together can't wait for the trip to end to be rid of each other? It is an incurable problem, but not a serious one.

"Make Sari stop singing."

What to do?

Same as always: Be sympathetic, but don't intervene.

"Gosh, I'm sorry it bothers you."

"But you have to make her stop."

At this point Max's father has nothing more to say. If Max persists, "You have to stop her. I can't think," he needs to be very firm.

Max's father's involvement with his son over Sari's singing has ended. And as always, the clearer Max's father is that Max will get nothing further out of him, the sooner Max will withdraw.

And if Max then returns to his sister, "Stop it! Stop it!"

"I can sing if I want to."

"No, you can't. It's driving me crazy."

"That's not my problem, is it?"

"Daddy said you had to stop."

"And I really believe you."

Maybe they work it out. Max moves elsewhere, or perhaps Sari gets bored with singing.

Or maybe they don't. A fight ensues, at which point their father—if the fighting bothers him—intervenes to separate them. But he does not touch the issue of singing.

But Sari should have a right to sing. Their father should stop Max from fussing whenever Sari wants to sing. It's not fair to squelch her happiness and maybe even her creativity.

If crabby brothers actually had this power, it would be a reason for concern. But fortunately, the reality is that crabby brothers do not impede singing careers or expressions of happiness. Sari will continue to sing—because she likes to, maybe even further inspired by her brother's reaction.

I love to sing. I also love how Max goes crazy.

And many years later: "I am proud to accept this Golden Elmer Career Singing Award. I owe my career to my brother. As a child I loved to sing. But I *really* loved how it drove him crazy. Thank you. Thank you so much."

The other reality—no way around it—is that any intervention both pulls their father in and goes nowhere good.

"Max, you have to understand that Sari is only being happy. She is not doing it to you."

"You're always on her side."

"I'm not on anyone's side. You have to understand that your sister likes to sing and singing is good. You can sing."

"I hate singing and singing is stupid and she is doing it to bother me. You don't know."

Other People's Children

Part of the following story is true, part of it is not. I leave it to you to discern which is which.

Mary Alice and I were lucky. Nick and Margaret were generally pretty good in restaurants. Taking them out in public was something we almost always enjoyed. I was actually proud of how Nick and Margaret were kids we could take out, go places with. But certainly they were not perfect.

One time when Nick and Margaret were maybe seven and nine, we were in a restaurant. At a table next to us was a family with two children, a boy and a girl, who looked to be about the same age as Nick and Margaret. Over the course of our meal, I kept glancing over at the family. I could not help noticing how well behaved the two children were. They did not fuss, but neither were they rigid. They seemed relaxed, having a good time. Not only that, both kids eagerly joined into conversation with their parents. And not only that, I couldn't help but notice what good table manners they had.

As I said, I had always been rather proud of how good Nick and Margaret were in public, patting myself on the back over how they behaved. But this family presented a whole other order of child restaurant behavior. The more I watched, the less good I felt about my own parenting. I was embarrassed for my children, but especially embarrassed about my inferior parenting skills, now realizing what could be achieved.

We were still finishing our meal when the other family left, but by then I was really quite depressed, questioning everything about myself. *I'm a fraud. I'm a failure.*

Then a funny thing happened. From where I was seated I could see the parking lot exit and the stretch of road that led away from the restaurant. What I saw was the family getting into their car, driving off down the road, but then the car simply evaporating into thin air. Obviously I was mystified. But then I realized what had happened. This was not a family in which the parents possessed superior child-raising skills, not at all. It was a family put there by the devil. It was one of those families whom His Supreme Evilness regularly places in restaurants in order to accomplish precisely what in this case it so successfully did—make normal parents feel woefully inadequate about their parenting.

There is a serious side to this story, which is that we do the best we can with our children. We try to have our kids get along with each other, show generosity, look out for each other. Most of the time we feel okay about our kids. But it is inevitable that you will know or will come into contact with families where—at least from what you see—they seem to be especially nice to each other, well behaved in a way that you never see with your own kids.

"Why can't the two of you act like Rebecca and Anton?"

"Because they're spoiled, stuck-up babies who get everything they want."

It makes you feel badly; makes you feel less competent as a parent.

I don't know what Jay and Karen do right, but it must be something because Rebecca and Anton are always so nice to each other. I wish I could do something to make that happen with Zachary and Neil.

My only point: Because your children are human children, they come with many flaws. This can be especially apparent at certain times when you compare them to others. You are not always going to feel good about what you have accomplished. You will question your parenting. At times uncertainty cannot be avoided. It comes with being a parent.

Real Inequalities

The Star

Tiffany could do everything well. A voice like a nightingale. A natural soccer player. A's across the board in school. And of course, lovely to look at. People on the street often would say as they passed, "What a lovely girl." Then there was Tiffany's two-years-older sister Desiree. School was always a struggle for Desiree, what with her serious reading disability for which she had to get special help. Desiree sang, but it was always off-key. Unfortunately, she just wasn't very coordinated. Sports, dancing, karate—none came easily to her. She was not ugly. In truth, Desiree's looks weren't exactly anything—what they used to call "plain." People passing in the street would often say, "What girl? I didn't notice." That is, you name it, Tiffany was head and shoulders better at it, more blessed than Desiree.

Two Desirees in two separate but parallel universes.

—Universe 1—

"I can't wait for Tiffany's concert. I'm so excited for her. Imagine, there's actually going to be someone from a recording company there to hear her. I am so excited."

"Excuse me."

"Yeah?"

"You're excited for Tiffany?"

"Yeah."

"You, who didn't make the chorus for your second-grade musical *The Happy Maple Tree*?"

"Yeah, why wouldn't I be excited? She's my sister."

"You don't feel a little jealous?"

"No. I mean sure, I wish I could sing as well as her. I would love that. But I can't."

"You're not at least a little bitter toward her? She's always the star, and never you."

"But it's good. At least we have one star in the family."

—Universe 2—

"I can't wait for Tiffany's concert. I'm so excited. Imagine, there's actually going to be somebody from a recording company there to hear her. I can't wait. Imagine how humiliated that little bitch will be when her throat suddenly seizes and all she can do is squawk because of the chemical I have been preparing in the middle of the night and will drop in her lemonade just before she goes out on-stage."

The above story is perhaps a bit overstated. Nonetheless, it does reflect a reality. There can be, and often are, major differences in the levels of accomplishment and overall attractiveness—at least in the eyes of the outside world—of different siblings. But also, given these differences, there can be altogether different reactions from the less talented, less attractive sibling as to how hurt or not she feels in regard to her less naturally blessed status. Further, some of those attitudinal differences can be a result of their innate temperament. But much has to do with how their parents handle it.

Let me tell another story, one that may be somewhat familiar.

There was this girl, Cynthia, who had two older sisters named Grendel and Ashwig. Cynthia's parents deeply loved the two older sisters and spoiled them rotten. They got all kinds of fancy clothes. Every afternoon they were served a wonderful tea with delicate pastries. They never had to do a lick of work. On the other hand, Cynthia's parents never paid any attention to her, gave her only rags to wear, and made her do all the nasty jobs around the house like sweeping the ashes from the fireplace. By the way, Cynthia was the natural child of the parents, not a stepdaughter.

Growing up, how would Cynthia feel? For one thing, Cynthia was attached to her parents—even the scorned cannot help it—and as a result, her parents were for her the primary givers of worth and value. Since they obviously did not value her, Cynthia could only feel less about herself, that in some innate way she was a second-class being. Also, she felt envy, real resentment, toward her sisters, as witnessed by her constantly smuggling copies of *Cinderella* into the house—before they were confiscated by her parents—and always underlining the part where Cinderella's sisters chop off their own toes to try to fit into the glass slippers.

My point is an obvious but important one. The piece of a child's self-worth that is acquired at home comes from the parents' attitude toward their child, not from how that child's accomplishments compare to those of a sibling. If children feel that their parents care about them equally, that they on their own are seen as special, then relative levels of accomplishment have little meaning in the context of home and family.

How is the above accomplished? By making sure that each child gets special attention for what they do—not in comparison to a sibling—but for them.

Mom and Dad really listened to my song when I tried out for The Happy Maple Tree. *They thought I was good. Too bad I didn't make it into the show.*

The parents' message must be that all are equally special.

Tiffany is great at stuff, but Mom and Dad love me as much as they love her.

Not So Good

Jeffrey and his mother were in the kitchen when the phone rang.

"Oh, hi, Mom. Guess what? I couldn't wait to tell you. Randall, Mr. Whiz Kid, did it again. He got a second place in the all-state math contest, and the other kid had math tutoring since he was two."

The conversation went on for a while, elaborating Randall's accomplishments. No mention was made of Jeffrey.

The next afternoon, the mother's good friend Ruthie dropped over at the house.

"Ruthie, I couldn't wait to tell you. Mr. Whiz Kid, Randall, got a second in the state math contest. He is something else."

Standing next to her was Jeffrey. In the conversation that followed, again no mention was made of him, but much was made of his brother.

Jeffrey, Randall, and their mother were at the supermarket when they ran into Rudy, an old family friend.

"How's it going, guys? Hi, Evelyn. How's it going?"

"Rudy, you won't believe it. Randall, Mr. Whiz Kid, did it again . . ." And she again described Randall's success. Again no mention was made of Jeffrey.

"Excuse me. Excuse me."

"What *is* it Jeffrey?"

"I made a kaka on purpose in the bathtub this morning and it's still there."

It is good to recognize and be excited for their accomplishments. It is also necessary to be aware of the other children in the family.

Mom thinks he is more special. Mom thinks I am less special.

They will feel this way.

In talking to others, friends, family, even at home, you want to make a conscious effort to talk of all the kids. Further, too much praise of one is not especially useful to the one praised, either. He loves it—but *If I screw up, do I lose my special status in their eyes?*

Probably. Children do not need that pressure.

Also, too much focus at the expense of others promotes a distorted view of the self.

I am more special than others. Others—for example, my sister Frances—do not deserve as much as me.

This is not good.

Unequal Love

"You love Sissy more than me," sobbed Naomi, furious at her mother because she, Naomi, got yelled at for making a big fuss while they were waiting in line at the supermarket.

I can't help it. Naomi is right. I do love Sissy more than her. I mean, I love Naomi, I really do. But it's not the same as with Sissy. Sissy was my first, and right from the start I just felt this special bond with her. It's like I identify with her. I want everything for her. She's my treasure. She's always been. I love Naomi, too, but it's never been the same as with Sissy.

Isn't it the law that you have to love all your children equally? Isn't it true that if you genuinely love one sibling more than another, there is something very wrong with you? Won't your less loved child be severely damaged?

Not really. Each child is different. Each child comes in at a different point in our lives. Usually we do *not* feel the same about each of our children. We have a different history with each. And each can have a different meaning to us, especially as to where we were in our lives.

"With Alex I was so absorbed with work and making sure I got ahead so that I could support the family. I left all the parenting to Cindy. But with Kane I had more time; I've always had much more of a relationship with him. To be honest, I've thought of Alex more as Cindy's child than mine. But it's not at all like that with Kane."

A child reminds you of a parent who died and whom you loved. A child reminds you of a parent who died and whom you hated.

We love them differently. Sometimes we even love one more. This is normal and not necessarily a problem.

It is a problem only if our actions too clearly reflect a preference. It is useful to recognize, to admit to yourself, that the feelings may be different. This allows you to do the one thing that is necessary: As best you can, show them equal love. Give them time, affection, encouragement. It may not turn out to be completely equal, but from their standpoint that is almost always good enough. Fortunately, the vast majority of children assume that their parents love them and their siblings the same.

"Do you love Paul and Carlos the same?"

"No. Paul has always been warm, affectionate, and open. Carlos has always been more moody, and he pulls into himself, is often unresponsive when I try to be close with him. I have always tried to show both of them the same amount of love, but the truth is, Paul gets much more of me because he is so much more responsive, easier to love."

We look at videotapes of the time their mother spends with her two sons. It is obvious that she does spend more one-on-one time with Paul, and though we can see that she is nice to Carlos, that she genuinely does try to reach out to him, she is very different with the two boys, noticeably happier, clearly enjoying her interactions with Paul.

We ask Paul and Carlos.

"Does your mother love you the same?"

Paul: "Yes, she loves us both the same."

Carlos: "Yes, she loves us both the same."

We hook them up to lie detectors.

"Do you really believe that your mother loves you both the same?"

Both repeat that they think she does, and the lie detector indicates that they are telling the truth.

Children desperately need to believe that they—by their

birthright—are the recipients of full, unconditional parent love. Fortunately, if you regularly try to show them love, they will assume that they are getting their fair share—because they want to and because it is too disturbing not to.

After getting yelled at, Naomi may well bemoan, "You love Sissy more than me."

But it is in anger to get back at her mother, not because she believes it.

But it's terrible. I do love Sissy more than Naomi. I feel so bad for Naomi, but I can't help it. It's what is in my heart. I feel bad for Naomi. It's so sad.

Not really, unless Naomi's mother tells her.

"Naomi, sweetheart, I feel I have to be honest. Mommy does love Sissy more than you."

Which of course Naomi's mother should never do.

You do not have to worry about loving them equally because you cannot. You love each of them differently. They are different. And that is fine.

The Difficult Child

"But why? But why? Why? I changed my mind. I don't want chocolate. I want pistachio."

"No, Ben, you had your chance. We're not going to buy you another cone."

"Then I don't want this fucking cone," and Ben threw his cone across the Moo Moo Freeze parking lot, hitting the tire of a station wagon.

"Here, he can have the pistachio," volunteered a compassionate teenager at the service window.

Ben's parents briefly debated whether they should accept the offer. They decided they would, as they were not in the mood for another of Ben's protracted tantrums.

"Say thank you, Ben."

"Thank you."

Ben's two-years-older brother Lucas looked on quietly. Actually, Lucas, after getting his chocolate swirl cone, had seen someone with a pistachio and had thought of asking whether he might get a pistachio instead. But after Ben's scene, *No, I don't want to make a fuss.*

Some children are significantly more difficult than others. They seem to fill more time and space. They require more attention, more parent energy. And when the family is together, it almost invariably ends up being about them.

An interview with Lucas:

"Do you mind that Ben gets so much more attention?"

"Not really. He can't help it. I get mad at him sometimes, but mainly I just try to stay out of his way. But I do get mad that he causes Mom and Dad so much trouble. After Mom had her operation and she was home from the hospital, he didn't even let up then.

"Sometimes I stand up to him. I can beat Ben up. But usually I'll let him have what he wants because it's too much effort not to. He just doesn't stop, he just keeps coming. I know he's on medication. I wish it worked better."

The boys' father:

"I do feel bad for Lucas. Despite what he says, it's not

fair to him. Ben gets so much more attention, and I can see that Lucas just stays out of his way.

"Over spring vacation, Ben went to stay with my sister and his cousin who live in Florida. It's really sad to say, but when Ben was away the house was so much more peaceful. I hate to say it because it upsets me, but with Ben out of the house for a week, Lucas seemed more bubbly, happier."

What should a parent do if there is a child who because of constant difficult behavior ends up getting a disproportionate amount of attention and energy? Is it fair to the other children? No. Can it have a negative effect on them? Yes. Nonetheless, there are things you can do that make a big difference in whatever negative effects might occur.

For one, make sure that you regularly have one-on-one time with those who may not be getting their full share of you. It does not have to be big chunks of time. They nonetheless like it a lot.

Ben hogs everything, but I still get my time with Dad.

Second, regularly make a point of talking with them. Recognize for them what it must be like. Do this even if they deny that it is an issue.

"I know because of the way he is, Ben gets a lot of our attention. Sometimes it has to make you feel kind of cheated and maybe mad at him, or maybe mad at us that he is always the center of everything."

Maybe, "I do. He should stay in Florida next time."

Or, "No, it's no problem. I don't mind."

But they do mind, and it is important that you let them know that you know that at least sometimes they feel this way and that it is okay.

This does not solve the problem of having an attention-dominating sibling who can and does change a household, often not for the better. But guaranteeing that everyone else will get their time and recognizing how they feel can make a real difference.

A Bad Influence?

Gareth, now a teenager, had been more than difficult for years. His parents had learned from experience to pick their battles. One battle they had long ago given up on was his mouth.

"Gareth, I need you to help clean out the garage."

"I'm not going to clean up any of that fucking shit."

"Gareth, we need you to help."

"Fuck that shit."

"Gareth, we need your help."

As his parents had learned, if they didn't starting yelling at him about his mouth and his attitude, he often—as he did in this instance—ended up doing what they asked.

Four days later Gareth's father came to his ten-year-old son Dwayne.

"Dwayne, please hang up all the coats and sweaters that are on the hall closet floor."

"I'm not going to clean up any of that fucking shit," said Dwayne, who had been right there when his older brother had used those exact same words in response to the request to help clean out the garage.

This is a real concern of parents: the older, naughtier one influencing the younger.

Well, he hears Gareth talking that way, and we can't really do anything to stop it. We hate it, but we have to live with it. But I'll be damned if I'm going to let Gareth get away with turning Dwayne—who has never been a bad kid, and who really doesn't use that kind of language—into somebody who acts like Gareth. One is enough.

It is a legitimate concern, and fortunately there is an answer. Gareth is Gareth and Dwayne is Dwayne. That is, Gareth is a difficult kid; Dwayne really has not been. Yes, Dwayne is copying Gareth. He thinks it's cool to talk that way. He hears Gareth talking in a surly manner and nothing much seems to happen to him because of the bad language. So he tries it.

The difference is that because he is not Gareth, what will not work with Gareth will work with him.

"What did you say?"

"I said I don't want to do the closet," said Dwayne in a surly tone but already backing off from the language in the confrontation with his father. Dwayne does not have the permanent ax to grind, the chip on his shoulder that is part of his brother's makeup. The same response to Gareth would have gotten, "I said I'm not going to clean up any of that fucking shit," this time especially emphasizing the swear words.

Dwayne's swearing is coming from a very different, far more benign place than his brother's. And the parent intervention that long ago failed with Gareth will far more likely work with Dwayne.

Later, to Dwayne, "I really don't like you using that kind of language with me."

"But Gareth says stuff like that all the time and you don't do anything to him."

His parents do not want to touch the comparison.

"I do not want to hear that kind of language from you."

Difficult children can influence the behavior of their siblings. But they are not them. Unless the personalities of the two are similar to begin with, what did not work in changing the unwanted behavior of the problem child will nonetheless work just fine with the other sibling.

Some Family Issues

More Than Two—Larger Families

Hunter wanted to be on the slide. Kerry wouldn't give him a turn. Douglas started bossing Kerry, telling him to give Hunter a turn. Kerry pushed Douglas, who accidentally stepped on Tina's sand castle.

"Mom, Kerry won't let me on the slide."

"Mom, Kerry pushed me."

"Mom, Douglas won't mind his own business."

"Mom, Douglas wrecked my sand castle on purpose."

"I have a plan," said the children's mother. "Let's all take naps. Now is the perfect time for all of us to take very long naps."

"But I don't want a nap."

"We already had two naps."

"Yes, long naps. Just the ticket," said their mother.

Throughout this book, most of the examples I give are of two siblings. What about larger families, or situations involving more than two? Often with larger families, bickering is between two, but sometimes it can be more, which can make it tougher. What to do?

The answer is simple. For almost all day-to-day bickering, the same rules apply. Don't intervene on anyone's side, and don't listen.

If the four are playing outside and nobody seems in danger of getting hurt, one good option for the children's mother is not to get involved at all.

"Mommy."

"Mommy."

"Mommy."

"Mommy."

"You'll just have to work it out yourselves."

"But . . ."

"But . . ."

"But . . ."

"But . . ."

"You'll just have to work it out yourselves. But would anybody like a hug?"

"No."

"No."

"Yes."

"I don't know. I think I just swallowed a bug. I think maybe I need the Heimlich maneuver."

On the other hand, if the bickering seems to be verging on out-of-control, or it has crossed over your aggravation threshold, the next option is to separate them. With multiple children, this becomes a little more complicated, but not impossible. A good strategy—which relies on your knowledge of your children—is to make swift decisions about removing one or two from the scene.

"Kerry and Douglas, I want you over here near me or you can go in the house. You've had enough time on the climbing set."

"But I didn't do anything. It's not fair."

"I don't care what you did or didn't do. I want you and Kerry away from the slide for now."

You want to act quickly, not listening to what went on, not acting as judge, not assessing fault or wrong, and hence not letting yourself get sucked into the middle.

I don't like what is going on and so now I am going to act swiftly to change that.

"But it's not fair."

"It's not fair."

"I like it."

"So do I."

"Hunter and Tina like it, that's not fair."

With bickering that involves more than two, it is more difficult because there are more of them. But the basic rules do not change. And as with two siblings, they do learn.

Either we work it out on our own, or if we can't, then Mom or Dad will intervene, but they're not going to listen, and we have to take our chances.

But Daddy Said We Could

"What are you three doing?"

"Watching TV."

"I said I didn't want any of you watching TV this afternoon. No TV. No video games. It's a beautiful day. I want all of you outside."

"But Daddy said it was okay."

"Hank, did you tell the children it was okay for them to watch TV?"

"I guess so. What's the big deal?"

"I expressly told them not to. It's a beautiful day. I want them outside."

"How was I supposed to know?"

———

"Roddy, Rose, Raphael, I want the TV off. Now."

"But Daddy said it was okay. Didn't you, Dad? Mom, it's not fair. Daddy said it was okay."

"I want this room picked up by the time I get back from my haircut in an hour." Their father exits and drives off in his car.

"Mom"—who did not hear what their father said before he left—"do we have to pick up the family room now? We're just going to mess it up again. We'll do it this afternoon. Okay?"

"I guess so. This afternoon will be okay."

An hour later, their father returns from getting his hair cut. "Why isn't this room picked up?"

"Mom said we didn't have to."

"Mom, can we have ten dollars for lunch when we're at the mall?"

"No, you can eat when you get home."

"Sidney"—the twins' stepfather—"can we have ten dollars for lunch at the mall?"

"I guess so."

"Better make it fifteen. Lunch can be pretty expensive."

"Oh, okay."

———

When there is more than one parent in the home, it is the rare child who does not look for the best deal. This does not mean that your kids are going to grow up to be con men (or women) or tax cheats. It's what children do. The only serious problem arises when it creates friction between the parents. Fortunately, there are basic rules that can help where children seek to play one parent against the other.

Ideally, you would communicate: "Claire, is it okay with you if the kids watch TV?" or "Jack, I told the kids I want them outside this morning, not watching TV."

For major issues, communication is essential. But most often in real life, moment-to-moment decisions are not checked with your partner. It is inconvenient and, besides, parents should be free to make unilateral decisions in regard to their children without always having to check with their spouse. But that opens the door for potential deviousness.

If you do check and it turns out there were conflicting instructions, you should discuss the situation *briefly* with the other parent, but in general the initial ruling should stand.

"Claire, I don't have a problem with them watching TV."

"No, I definitely want them outside."

Parents must back each other up. If they truly disagree, they still need to decide fast which decision stands now. Later they can argue about the decision for future situations.

If the other parent is not available to check with, what you say goes.

"But Dad said we could leave doing it until tonight. Call him."

"No. I want it picked up now."

"Call him!"

"I'm not calling your father. I am the parent who is here, and you're stuck with what I say."

"But it's not fair. Call Dad. Call him."

If the children do manage to get away with their deception, confront them.

"You knew I said no eating cupcakes before dinner. I don't like your going around me to your father."

"But he said it was okay."

"You heard what I said."

Beyond the above, do you want to make a big deal about their deviousness? You have made it clear that you don't like it. But do you want to treat them as aspiring felons and make an even stronger statement so that they won't grow up to be criminals? With honesty—similar to fairness, discussed earlier—your main influence comes not from what you say, but from how honestly you deal with them and how honestly they see you deal with others. If occasionally they are successful at going around one parent and getting a better deal from the other, who cares?

Stepsiblings

Robert, Molly, Devon, and Lee were watching TV.

"Lee, stop switching the channels. Give me the remote," said Robert.

"You just want to watch *Growing Up with Reggie*, and I hate it."

"Give him the remote," said Molly.

At that point Lee and Devon's mother, Amanda, came into the room.

"Stop the fussing. Robert and Molly, let Lee keep the remote."

"You can't tell us what to do. You're not our mother," said Robert and Molly simultaneously. "Besides, this is our house."

Four months earlier, Amanda and her two children had moved in to live with Jim, Robert and Molly's father. Jim and Amanda had been seeing each other for about a year prior to Amanda's moving in. Robert and Molly had an older sibling, Denise, who lived with their mother and visited every other weekend. Robert and Molly saw their mother on alternate weekends. There was also one-year-old Lenny, their half brother by their mother and her current husband, Cal. Actually, for the most part, the two sets of siblings liked each other—though the house was now cramped, and with limited space bickering was common.

Three months later Jim and Amanda had a major falling-out, resulting in Amanda and her children abruptly leaving. Jim and Amanda never got back together. The two sets of children did not subsequently see each other, except for Molly and Devon, who were a year apart at the same school. They remained friendly but had no contact outside school.

Is what I just described a little confusing?

One reality in today's world is that for many children, what constitutes the family is far more fluid and complex than in past generations. I will not try to describe all the complexities that come into play when a sibling is neither a full-blood relative nor full-time in the home. Nonetheless, a basic fact is that when children are at home with a parent, the immature side of their personality—the baby self—tends to come out. This means that the basic rules for sibling bickering already described apply with stepsiblings as well.

But there are also major differences. Parent and stepparent are not the same. The conflicts that arise in the parenting of stepsiblings can be the source of serious difficulty between the adults, sometimes even resulting in the breakup of the relationship.

Again, if you follow certain guidelines, you can head off some of the most frequent problems.

As with full parents, when one parent is in charge at a given moment, the other parent must back him or her up, even if there is disagreement. Imagine the likely scenario with Robert and Molly, where Amanda intervened to let her son, Lee, keep the TV remote control.

Robert and Molly run to their father. "Dad, Amanda butted in and it was none of her business and she always wants to protect Lee."

Their father at that moment must back Amanda. If not, he undermines her authority, which will create great resentment in Amanda. If he disagrees with what she did, he can discuss it with her later, for future occasions. But he should not intervene now. The rule has to be that both adults must be treated as authority figures in the home.

But—and this is the major difference between step-parents and biological parents—on overall policy issues in regard to a given child, the natural parent has the final say. The adults *are not equal* in authority. The exception to this is if a stepparent has been part of the home since a child was very young and does have full-parent status—where the attachment between child and parent and child and stepparent is basically the same. Otherwise, the final say on rules, on policy for a given child, resides with the natural parent. The frequent stepchild complaint, "You're not my parent," does have validity. The relationship between child and parent has a history, a commitment, an attachment, a love, that is just not the same as with a stepparent.

When a stepparent is the sole adult in charge at the time, he or she should have full authority.

Ralph to his daughter and two stepchildren: "I've had it with your bickering. I want all of you in your rooms, now."

"But Mom said we could stay up and watch *Tiger Tales*."

"I don't care what your mother said. She's at work and I'm the one in charge here. You're making too much noise."

Their mother does need to back up this decision when—guaranteed—her children later complain

"He's the boss of Monica, but he has no right to boss us around. Besides, you said we could watch *Tiger Tales*."

"When it's just Ralph, he's in charge."

For overall rules and policy issues, the natural parent needs to have the last word.

Can her kids have friends over next Friday?

Do they have to finish all their vegetables in order to get dessert?

Can they watch the rerun of *Vampire's Revenge*?

And especially, anything that has to do with punishment or not.

It gets more complicated. What if there are different sets of rules within the same home?

Kelly and Candace, who are the same age, have different bedtimes. Or Kelly's mother will let her rent and watch *Death in the City*, but Candace's father feels it is not appropriate for a child her age. What should you do? There are two answers.

One is that there can be different rules.

Candace's complaint, "But it's not fair Kelly gets to stay up half an hour later and she's exactly my age," consistently gets nowhere with her father.

"That's nice for Kelly, but I'm your parent and I'm the one who makes the rules."

Candace won't like the inequality, but she will accept it. *Kelly is so lucky she has a nice mother. I wish she were my mother—at least for renting movies.*

Still, different rules for different children in the same household can be awkward. If Kelly gets to watch *Death in the City*, does that mean that Candace has to stay out of the room where the good TV is the whole time that Kelly is watching it? Often it is necessary for the parents to compromise. Maybe Kelly doesn't get to watch *Death in the City*.

"But it's not fair. Just because Gene doesn't want Candace to watch it shouldn't mean I can't watch it."

Sometimes these kinds of concessions have to be made. But if so, the child's complaint needs to be recognized. Especially since, in this case, Kelly is right—it isn't fair.

"You're right. If it was just you and me, I would let you watch it. But it's not."

"Everything sucks since they live here. I can't do anything."

"You're right that there are some changes that are not nice for you, and I'm sorry. But this is what I want"—that is, having Gene and his two children live with them. "You'll just have to live with it. I know it wasn't your choice, but it's what I want."

Candace's mother is recognizing two points: The new living arrangement does have some losses for Candace, and the choice to make that change was for the benefit of the mother, not Candace. It is important that parents recognize for their children that some of their grievances about a changed household are valid.

Children complaining about a new stepmother in the house:

"Since Janice moved in, she's a nut and she's always bugging us about pick up this and pick up that. Her kids are used to it, so it's not a big deal for them. But when it was just us and you, it was never like this."

Which may be true, and does represent a change.

"You're right. I never made you three do much at all. But Janice wants a much neater house than what we had, and I don't think it will kill you to learn to do a better job of picking up after yourselves."

With stepsiblings living in the home together, there usually are house rules. These rules should be the same for all children. Can food be eaten in the family room? How loud can music be played? Can shoes be left in the hallway? Equal assignment of household chores.

These rules must be negotiated between the two parents. Here compromise is almost always necessary, as their respective ideas about parenting and how houses should be run are probably not the same. Also, any agreed-upon rules may represent an unwelcome change for at least some of the children. Nonetheless, compromise is essential. If two adults—both with their own children—decide to live together, part of that plan has to include compromise. They must recognize that because they both have kids—who have been raised under different sets of rules—their choice to live together means that they have to give up some of the total control of their own children.

Big trouble can come if a stepparent tries to change the partner's children. First, it almost never works. Second, it creates resentment from the children. But the biggest problem is the resentment it creates in the natural parent.

He's not their father. Who does he think he is coming in and wanting to change my kids? I know they're not perfect, and I know they make mistakes, but they're my kids and I think they're great. I don't think I've done such a bad job.

The girls walk all over Evie. She doesn't see what little brats she's making them into. But she won't hear a word of it.

My Nancy and Danielle are completely different from Greg's kids. Besides, Roy and Anitra were raised completely differently from my two. I've raised Nancy and Danielle how I feel is right. But Greg doesn't see that at all. He just keeps comparing them to his own two, which is unfair.

If the natural parent goes along with it, if he or she really feels that the suggested changes are good, that's fine.

Greg says I should be tougher with the girls, and I agree. I know they resent it, but I do think it's what's best for them.

But that usually isn't the case. The rule for stepchildren is that in a decision for two adults to live together, the stepchildren are part of that—*the way they are,* not the way the new partner wants them to be. If Greg absolutely can't stand seeing how the two girls behave, the little monsters he feels their mother is making them, he doesn't have to live there.

———

The parenting of stepsiblings definitely adds a whole new level of complexity to the child-raising process. Nonetheless, the basic sibling rules described in this book—with the modifications just discussed—can go a long way toward making even these more complicated relationships far easier to manage.

Conclusion

"What are you doing?"

"We're playing together."

"You're doing what?"

"We're playing together."

"Alvie, why aren't you hitting your sister?"

"We already did that. Now we're playing."

"But what about me?"

"What about you?"

"Why aren't you coming to me?"

"For what?"

"For, you know, for bickering solutions."

"We're in charge of that."

"But I'm lonely."

"Oh, okay, if you really want us to."

"Mom, Alvie scuffed my shoe on purpose."

"I did not."

"Look at it, Mom."

"I didn't do it. You always blame me for everything."

"Was that good, Mommy?"

"Oh, yes. Thank you, children. I feel so much better, so much more needed."

"Anytime. Just let us know."

Maybe I should take up crocheting.

A last warning: Don't expect that when your children are finally grown up they will actually behave like grown-ups.

Patricia, her six siblings, and their significant others assemble at their mother's home several times a year for holidays, birthdays, anniversaries, and other special family events. They get along remarkably well, and no one minds that Patricia is a strict vegetarian—no one, that is, except her brother Grant. Every dinner, without fail, Grant swirls his fork around in his meat and gravy and then jabs it into Patricia's vegetables.

"Mommmmmmm!"

About the Author

ANTHONY E. WOLF, PHD., is a practicing clinical psychologist and the author of several books, including the bestselling *"Get out of my life, but first can you drive me and Cheryl to the mall?"*: *A Parent's Guide to the New Teenager, The Secret of Parenting,* and *"Why did you have to get a divorce? And when can I get a hamster?"* He has worked with children and adolescents for over thirty years and lectures widely on parenting topics. He lives in Suffield, Connecticut.

SIGRID ESTRADA